Hershey, Here!

At Saddle Up!

Crys Zinkiewicz

Hershey, Here!: at Saddle Up! / Crys Zinkiewicz

Copyright © 2016 by Crystal Zinkiewicz

All Rights Reserved. The purpose of this book is to raise both awareness of and funds for Saddle Up!, which is a non-profit therapeutic riding center serving children with disabilities. Anyone who, in lieu of making the purchase, copies the book, either in print or electronically, without the author's permission, is not only breaking the law but also taking funding away from this program and the children who benefit from it.

Cover and interior book design contributed by Marcia Myatt.

Photo Credits: Many of the photos have been pulled from Saddle Up!'s 2010–2015 archives. All of the photographers have graciously contributed their time and talent through the years to help Saddle Up! tell their story. Too often who to credit for a photo is simply no longer known—but still much appreciated! These photographers we do know—and also appreciate:

Susan Hay (cover 1, cover 4 both, pages 12, 14, 19, 20, 23, 31L top, 31R bottom, 38, 66, 82, 88L, 88R, 89, 104, 108, 109L, 110 middle)
Heather Silverman (10, 13, 16, 33, 41, 86, 97R top, 106, 115L)
Michael Shumate (36, 91, 92L, 92R, 98L, 102, 110L, 111L, 115R)
Gerald F. Plock (24, 45, 46, 76, 79L, 79R, 81R top, 81R bottom, 81L, 85, 105)
Nancy Swindell (8, 25, 34, 45 top, 46 top, 100)
Nichole Ochs (64, 65, 69, 71)
Martha Georgeson (73, 74)
Your Williamson staff (52, 111R, 120)
Derik Burrows (31L bottom)
Peyton Hoge (118)
Jennifer Krause (97 inset)
Krystin Krause (95R)
Maggie Moore (101)
Cheryl Scutt (17)
R. Shean (44)
Rick Stufflebean (119)
Lisa Wysoky (97L)

CONTENTS

Welcome to Saddle Up!
Meet Hershey 11

Pony Pal
Hershey & the Arena 15
    Saddle Up! Pony Pals 17
Hershey & the Bee 21
    Feeling Good 23

Therapeutic Riding
Hershey & the Games 29
    More Than Fun and Games 30
Hershey & the Not-So-Good Lesson 32
    On Lead/Off Lead 35
Hershey & the Big Baby 36
    Mom to the Rescue! 39
Hershey & the Meltdown 40
    Not Too Little 42
Hershey & the SUPER Show 44
    Everyone Is a Winner! 47

Equestrian Club
Hershey & "Pony Club" 50
    Saddle Up!'s Equestrian Club. 53
Hershey & the Cards. 54
    Learning to Care 55
Hershey & the Bucket List 56
    Empowering! 59
Hershey & the Music. 60
    Dancing Partners. 62

Equine Assisted Learning
Hershey & the Herd of Kids. 66
    Talking Ears 68
Hershey & the Hoof Picks 70
    Making Good Decisions. 72
Hershey & the Ball Game. 73
    Summer Fun at Saddle Up! 75

Therapy Services
Hershey & the Very Little Patient 78
    Walk Like Me. 80
Hershey & the Chimes 83
    The Fun Factor. 84
Second-Chance Lance 87
    Paddock, Pasture, and Tony Space. 88

Hershey's Herd

    Hershey & the New Arrival 90
        The Heart of the Matter 93
    Hershey & the Kiss 94
        Silver Slippers and So Much More 96
    Hershey & the Good-byes 98
        Where Do They Go? 99

Volunteers

    Hershey & the Paint Job 102
        Volunteering at Saddle Up! 103
    Hershey & Training the Volunteers 105
        Sleeping Horses 106
    Hershey & the Ghost 107
        The Black and White of It All 109

Ambassador

    Hershey & the Grand Prix 112
        Saddle Up! Ambassador 115
    Where Do the Funds Come From 116
        A Win/Win! 118
    Hershey Bar, Video Star 120

Just a Bit More

    Supporting the Mission 122
    PATH to Excellence 123
    Thank You! 124

Where all children are equal in the saddle

25 Years of Growth

Growth—Up and Up!

Volunteers — 4 to 500

Children — 10 to 250

Horses — 4 to 24

WELCOME TO SADDLE UP!

The hallmark of the 25-plus years of Saddle Up!'s existence has been growth:

- From four co-founders, all volunteers, to more than 500 volunteers donating about 17,000 hours a year

- From 10 children in a one-night-a-week, summer-only program to more than 250 children served six days a week year round

- From a borrowed farm to Saddle Up!'s own 34-acre farm and Americans with Disabilities Act (ADA)-compliant facility designed specifically for Saddle Up!'s programs

- From four borrowed horses to 24 dedicated horses, ponies, and miniature horses in Saddle Up!'s own herd

- From a single offering of therapeutic riding lessons to multiple programs: physical and occupational therapy, Equine Assisted Learning, Saddle Up!'s Equestrian Club, special summer weeks, and the foundational program of therapeutic riding—all of which are therapeutic ("good for you")

- From four volunteer riding instructors to 22 certified instructors and three professional therapists, two physical and one occupational

- From a dream of serving children with disabilities to accreditation as a Premier Accredited Center by the Professional Association of Therapeutic Horsemanship International (PATH, International), a designation earned by fewer than one-third of the member centers

But statistics only begin to paint the picture of this remarkable place. The heart of Saddle Up! shines through in the stories—of the children, their families, the volunteers, the staff, and the horses.

It's Hershey here to tell you some of those stories from his perspective as one of the horses living and working at Saddle Up!

Enjoy!

Where all children are equal in the saddle

MEET HERSHEY

Hershey, here.

Hershey Bar is my real name, but most people just call me Hershey. OK, some will go to Hersh. And a few call me Hershel—I just blow them off. I have one other name. Pal gave it to me. She calls me her Dark Chocolate Sweet Treat. I don't care about the dark chocolate part, but I perk up when I hear "treat"!

I know lots of words—"walk on," "whoa," "trot"—work words. But "treat," that's my favorite. Pal is pretty good about remembering the treat I like best—peppermint candy. But yesterday we'd finished our trail ride, and she started to lead me to the pasture. Well, I stopped! We were going the wrong way. I have horse sense. I know these things!

She had forgotten we're supposed to go to the Treat Place. *How could she!* So I stood my ground. She tried to get me to move, but I kept thinking, *Treat, treat, treat—that way, not this.* Finally, she said, "Oh, I bet you need a treat." Then I walked forward. We went to get my peppermint.

Ahhh. So good. That Pal, she can be really smart—sometimes.

Where all children are equal in the saddle

Hershey Bar

Breed: Quarter Horse
Color: Black
Markings: Star, Strip, Snip (Disconnected)
Height: 14.2 Hands
Birth Year: 1996
Background: Trail Horse
Came to Saddle Up! September 2010
Loves: Treats, especially peppermint candy
Hates: Having his left-front hoof cleaned

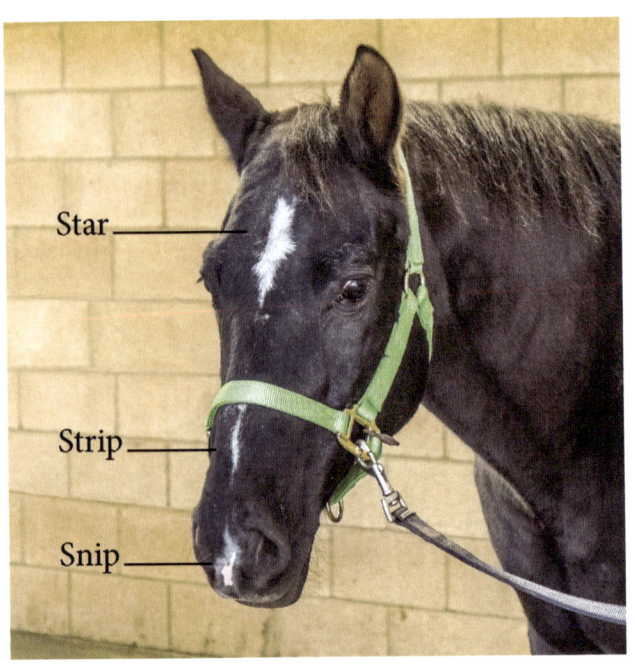

PONY PAL

HERSHEY & THE ARENA

Hershey, here.

I may have mentioned that the arena is not my favorite place. I am a *trail* horse! Nothing like a good trail ride.

When I first came to Saddle Up! I hated the arena. Round and round. Walk on. No— whoa! Stand around. (Well, that part was OK.) But we never went anywhere! Just more round and round.

I had to let those people know. So whenever I'd had enough, I nipped at the leader. *Someone should get the message!*

Then Pal came. I like Pal—she talks to me. I don't know everything she says, but the sound of her voice is musical. I can relax. And every once in a while, I hear the words that are truly music to my ears. "Hershey Bar, you are my Dark Chocolate Sweet Treat." I love it when she talks treat!

Pal was no pushover. (I don't like pushovers. How can I trust someone I can push around?) Pal took me into the arena—again and again. Round and round—again and again. Walk on and whoa—again and again. But my body was getting stronger. Turning was easier. Some things were starting to make sense.

More circles. Then came Figure 8s (that's two circles but opposite directions). Interesting. More walk on and whoa. Then, fast trot and slow trot. All right! Weave the cones. And then weave at a trot. *Definitely more fun!*

Where all children are equal in the saddle

OK, bring on the games! I can do this!

As she led me back to my pasture after our rides, Pal would keep talking. One day, I understood what she'd been saying week after week: "Hershey, Saddle Up! is a wonderful place to be. Here you have your herd buddies, plenty of food, and a good job. You have children who need you and who love you. Take care of your kids, Hershey. And take care of your leaders—no more nipping or you will have to leave."

Food, friends, kids who love me! I don't want to leave. Life is good at Saddle Up!

Pal, now can we go trail riding?

Cool Morning Ride

SADDLE UP! PONY PALS

Like Hershey, many of the horses at Saddle Up! have a volunteer Pony Pal. Once a week, sometimes twice, the Pony Pal works with his or her assigned horse for about an hour.

Sometimes the work is **conditioning**, getting the horse stronger and more supple. Just like people have to exercise, horses also need a workout. For some horses, the conditioning need is all over. When Lacy came to Saddle Up!, she was in very poor condition and needed gentle exercising to regain her strength.

Hershey was generally strong, but one-sided. Just as people favor a right hand or a left, horses are "handed." As a trail horse, Hershey could mostly use his favorite side. But in the arena he needed to use both. So, much of Pal's early work with Hershey was to get his muscles stronger on his "off" side, which helped him be more comfortable and confident doing whatever was asked of him.

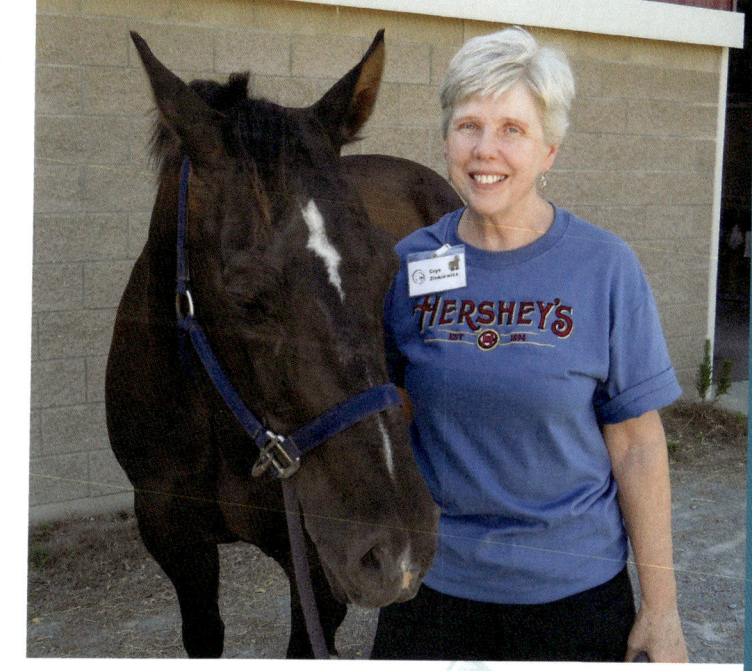

Every horse that comes to Saddle Up! has been trained and used—and a few, abused—in particular ways. Some were polo ponies; others were competitive show ponies. Some raced on the track; others "danced" in the dressage arena. Some ventured out into the world on different trails; others stayed safe in the world of their own pasture. Some had the advantage of good trainers; others not so much. Only two of them (Harley and Lucy) had done the particular kind of work asked of them at Saddle Up! **Training** the horses to be right for their new job is an ongoing part of the Pony Pals' responsibility.

All Saddle Up! horses, regardless of their background, breed, or temperament, need to be relaxed and easygoing. So **pampering** is also a Pony Pal task. Sometimes that means giving a horse extra brushing

Where all children are equal in the saddle

or a bath on a hot day. Sometimes it's a relaxing, fun ride out on the trails. Or, the horses' favorite, an extra treat.

Volunteers who apply to be Pony Pals have to pass a written quiz to show their knowledge of horses, and they must prove their abilities in a riding test. Only the best for the horses of Saddle Up!

Hershey's Places

Crossties

Inside the barn the horses are groomed and saddled (tacked up) and made ready for their lessons. The horse is led into an open stall area and turned to face outward. (As prey animals, horses prefer being able to see what's happening around them.) The leader will clip a tie (rope) to either side of the horse's halter. The crossties allow the horse to shift about comfortably, but not to wander off. The floor of the crosstie area is concrete, but large rubber mats cushion the horses so that standing there is not hard on them.

Arena

In contrast to the crosstie area, in the arena, where the horses are walking, trotting, and occasionally cantering, the floor is three to five inches of sand, soil, fibers, and recycled rubber bits, providing them with good footing that doesn't stress their joints. Taking care of the horses is a priority at Saddle Up! The arena, a large, enclosed oval, can accommodate multiple lessons at the same time. Outside is a second large arena with sand as the footing. The arena is sometimes referred to as "the ring."

Stop-and-Talk Spot

Anyone who has ever taken a riding lesson knows the Stop-and-Talk Spot. Usually, it's near the center of the ring or arena, but actually it's wherever the instructor is. At various points in a lesson the riders will be called to come closer to the instructor to receive... instructions. The horses soon learn the Stop-and-Talk Spot means they don't have to Go-and-Walk—at least for a few minutes. Break time!

Treat Place

According to Hershey, a treat place can be anywhere and anytime his favorite snack foods appear; the more the better! However, *the* Treat Place is the place he can count on for getting a treat. Horse treats—peppermints and apple-flavored "cookies"—are "behind Door #1," the office of the equine and farm staff.

Horses don't work for treats, and trainers do not use them as a training aid the way treats are sometimes used in working with dogs and other mammals. But horses do like treats, and they soon know exactly where they are and who has them. And with a big nudge the horses will let you know if you forget.

Treat Place

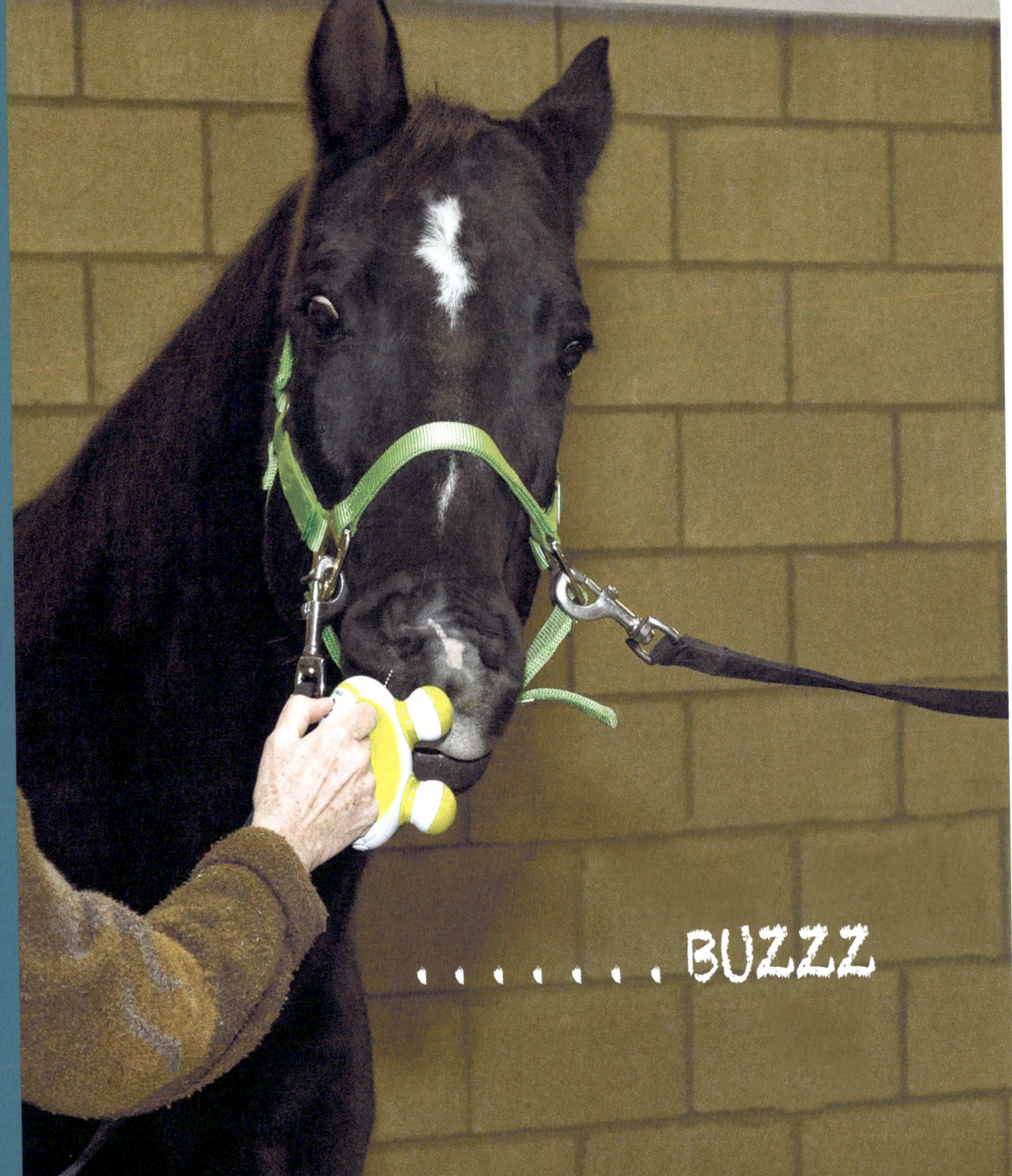

HERSHEY & THE BEE

Hershey, here.

Pal and I were on a trail ride—my favorite thing! Apache and Tommy and their Pals were along too. The weather was sunny and warm. I was enjoying life. But then... *Bees?! Did someone say, "Bees"? Oh, no!*

I remember bees from the old days—before Saddle Up! I had been on a trail then too. I was walking along, when my buddy just ahead suddenly went crazy. *What?!* He bucked. He crow hopped. He bucked again!

Then I knew "what"! Bees flew up from the ground and attacked me too! Lucky for me, my rider kicked his heels into my sides— "Get outa here!" I didn't have to be told twice! We ran.

Buddy wasn't so lucky. His rider thought he was acting out for no reason, so he tried to stop Buddy and correct him. Poor Buddy! He was covered with stings. (So was his rider!) Not me—only a few. But enough to not want to be stung ever again!

Fortunately, this time no bees ruined our trail ride. *Whew!*

Back at the barn Pal put me in the crossties, pulled off the saddle, and brushed. Then I heard her, "Hershey, I have a treat for you." *Pal, you're the best!*

"It's the bee."

Pal! That's no treat!

I moved away, but the crossties held me. Pal was coming at me with a... *bee?* "Look, Hershey, it's not a real bee." She held it for me to see. "It will make you feel really good."

It began to buzz. *Oh, no!* I stepped back as far as I could. But she put it on my side, and then on my back. *Oh, my!* This bee was definitely different. *Pal, move it over a bit. That's it, right there. Ahhh... I love a good massage.*

22.

FEELING GOOD

Hershey, of course, is right—bees are no treat, unless the bee is the cute, vibrating hand-held massage "bee" that occasionally visits the grooming area. Massage is one of several ways the Saddle Up! humans have of helping the horses feel good. The bee may come out; but a good pair of gentle hands works well too, and they're more readily available.

Sometimes when a horse seems stiff or sore, the staff will arrange for a professional massage, a full-body treatment. Most of the time, however, caring pony pals and leaders give mini-massages to their charges. A favorite place for horses is to be gently rubbed between the ears.

How do we know it's a favorite? The horses tell us—they relax and lower their heads, as if to say, *"I'll make that easier for you. Just keep doing what you're doing."* And they "lick and chew," moving their lips and tongue, as a person might who just had a really good bite of something sweet and wanted to get every last bit of flavor.

After a ride, when a rider dismounts, she or he runs up the stirrups onto the saddle (so they don't bang the sides of the horse) and then the instructor loosens the girth. The girth needed to be tight during the ride to keep the saddle—and rider—in place, but loosening it for the walk back to the grooming area makes the horse more comfortable. At that moment the horse will very likely "lick and chew" as if to say, *"Good ride, done. Time to relax."* That's a treat too.

Licking & Chewing

Therapeutic

"Good for you" describes the meaning of "therapeutic." In 1894 in *The Use of Life*, John Lubbock wrote, "There is nothing so good for the inside of a man as the outside of a horse." The certainty of those words applies not only to men but also to women, teens, and children. That truth has resonated through the years. Even British Prime Minister Winston Churchill and President Ronald Reagan have repeated the statement and been quoted for it. At Saddle Up! the "good-for-you" factor of being with the horses buoys the children and also the volunteers, many of whom come because the outside of a horse is therapeutic for them too.

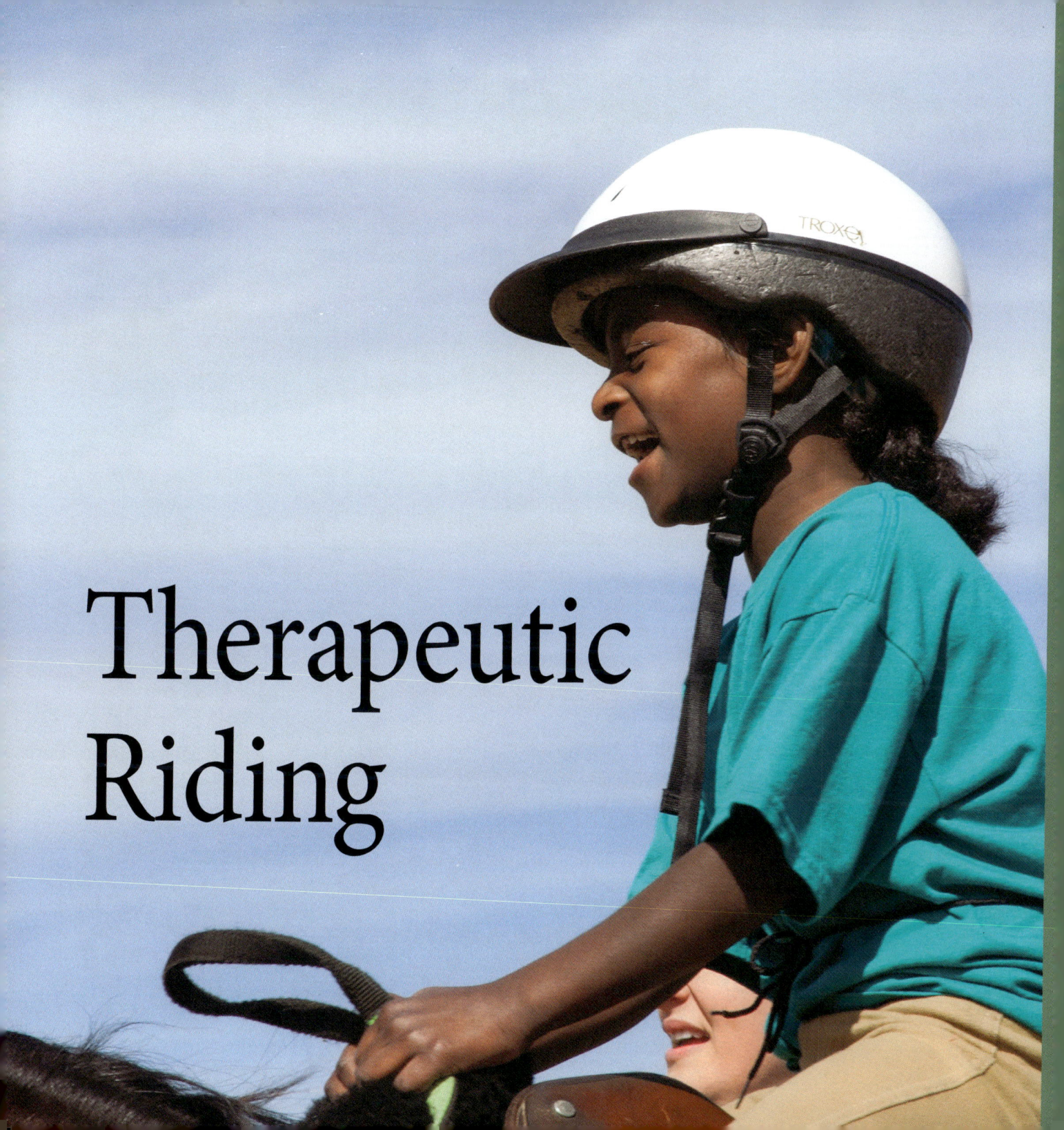

Therapeutic Riding

"Where all children are equal in the saddle"

Disabilities

In order to participate in any of the programs of Saddle Up!, the child must have a disability. The range of disabilities for body and brain is vast. Saddle Up! has documented over 60 specific ones among the children served through the years. Autism, cerebral palsy, Down Syndrome, chromosomal disorders, developmental delay, spina bifida, and attention-deficit/hyperactivity disorder are among the most frequent diagnoses. Saddle Up! instructors are trained to understand the safety and educational implications of the various disabilities. Their lessons and interactions show their knowledge as they teach, respond to, and care for their riders, students, and patients.

Abilities

The focus of Saddle Up!, however, is on *abilities,* rather than disabilities. As lessons progress, instructors and volunteers consistently see children growing in their abilities to understand, to focus, to communicate, to feel comfortable and confident, to interact both with their horse and with people as they also increase their abilities to ride and to care for their horse. At Saddle Up! the disability does not define the participant. Staff, instructors, and volunteers take their cues from the horses, who are completely nonjudgmental. For the horses "all children are equal in the saddle."

Non-verbal

Some of the riders at Saddle Up! are non-verbal. They may verbalize, making sounds but not words. Or their words may be minimal and elemental. But the experience with the horses is often a breakthrough. A child—who doesn't speak—suddenly and appropriately says, "Gok un." The sounds make meaning: "Walk on." Another child whose words are limited and barely spoken above a whisper chimes out, "Walk on!" As a mother and grandmother drive to Saddle Up! for the third lesson, their child in his car seat becomes excited as they near their destination. He suddenly bursts out with "Ride the pony!" It is his first full sentence. The stories speak. The stories reveal the heart of Saddle Up!

HERSHEY & THE GAMES

Hershey, here.

The arena is still not my favorite place, but most of the time it's a fun place. Whenever I walk in, I do a quick look-around. What's out there? Cones? Barrels? The basketball thing? Oh, good—we're playing games!

Walk-and-Whoa is really easy for me. Instructor holds up one sign and then the other. Rider is supposed to do whatever the sign and Instructor say. Sometimes Rider is pretty good at it; sometimes I take over. If I'm walking and the other sign goes up, I whoa. If I've stopped and the other sign flashes, I go. Pretty simple.

Same thing for the Music Game. Music plays, I start walking. Music stops, I stop. Sometimes I wait for Rider to tell me. Sometimes I just play the game.

Barrel-to-Rail is more challenging. Rider chooses something from the barrel, stuffs it someplace I can't see on the saddle (but I can feel it), and then we go find something else on the rail that matches. Whenever Rider finds the right thing, we whoa. Rider leans way over in the saddle to pick it up. If Rider is too far off balance, sometimes I shift over. I don't want Rider to fall. Pal says to take care of my kids. I try.

Last week I got a surprise. When I got to the rail, there was a saddle. *Hey! What's this doing here?* I nudged it with my nose. Sidewalker got a surprise too—it nearly fell!

I think I've just invented a new game!

MORE THAN FUN AND GAMES

Play is a natural way to learn. Games make learning play. Instructors at Saddle Up! carefully choose the day's games to help the riders work on basic riding skills, like walk and whoa, weaving (turning the horse right and then left), and posting (moving in rhythm with the horse's trot). Or the games may be aimed at more generalized skills, such as counting or matching colors, pictures, or parts of something. Playing the games also teaches life skills, such as listening, following directions, taking turns, working as a team.

Holiday seasons are especially fun at Saddle Up! Halloween, for example, brings out the fanciful and the "fearful" with crazy costumes and games like the Spoon and Eyeball Race, in which riders and horses go as fast as they can to the finish line, carrying a spoon with an appropriately decorated hardboiled egg! Who knows if it's the movement of the horse or the laughter of the riders that makes the "eyeballs" fall! Hershey loves Halloween lessons. The games finish with a treat! The riders take the horses to bob for apples.

The fun is what the riders enjoy, but the experience of riding week after week is also helping them in other ways. Bodies become stronger; balance is better; confidence grows.

The well-trained, caring, and creative instructors at Saddle Up! keep the fun factor high, but they especially look for—and cherish—all the ways the riders are learning.

Where all children are equal in the saddle

HERSHEY & THE NOT-SO-GOOD LESSON

Hershey, here — back in the arena. Most lessons are fine. Rider has fun. I have fun. I get a treat! *Pretty good.*

However...

One day, in the middle of a lesson, I hear "off lead." *Oh, good, something different.* Leader unhooks the lead rope from my halter and steps off to the side—not too far away. Rider is supposed to take charge.

We're just standing there. *I'm not getting any messages here.*

Leader steps closer and tugs my halter to say "walk on." OK. I start walking. *Hey, where am I supposed to go? I'm not getting any messages here! Hey, Rider, which way?* Still nothing.

I'm a good trail horse. I'll just follow the horse in front of me. Rider will figure it out.

OK, Rider, now what? I need direction here.

Not happening.

That's it! I'm done waiting. We'll do it my way!

I head straight for the Stop-and-Talk Spot in the center of the arena. *I'm done!*

Leader catches me and clips the lead rope back on. *OK, so I'm not done. But at least someone is in charge. I can relax again.*

Maybe, next time, Rider. We'll try again later.

34.

ON LEAD/OFF LEAD

Every Saddle Up! lesson has an instructor, who is certified, paid, and in charge. In addition, most every rider has at least one volunteer in the lesson. The "sidewalker" is responsible for the rider, keeping the child safe, assisting him or her in understanding instructions, and encouraging the young rider. Depending upon the type and level of disability, the rider may have either one or two volunteer sidewalkers. Independent riders usually do not need a sidewalker.

On the other hand, "leaders," who are also volunteers, are responsible for the horse or pony. In addition to making sure the horse is groomed and tacked up, the leader is right there, attached to the horse with the lead rope for both safety and direction. For riders who are not yet capable of managing the horse—even for walk on and whoa—the leader is the primary one communicating to the horse what is needed. As riders advance, they take on more of the directing of the horse both on lead and then off lead.

Horses *want* someone to be in charge. In the wild they run in herds with a stallion or an "alpha mare" telling the herd what to do. Domesticated horses continue to have that "herd mentality," which is one reason they form working relationships with humans. Someone else is in charge.

Horse and rider may only be a "herd of two," but the horse wants the rider to direct. Otherwise, as Hershey says, "We'll do it my way," which usually means a not-so-good lesson.

HERSHEY & THE BIG BABY

Hershey, here.

Shiloh can be such a baby! I was in a lesson with him one day. He was all about himself—not his job, not his rider.

First, he kept yelling for Ace. Ace is both his buddy and his brother. They look alike. I sometimes have to look twice at them to tell them apart. Except when Shiloh is acting out. Ace doesn't do that so much.

Next, Shiloh got antsy. You'd think he really did have ants all over him. But no. He was just being a big baby.

Leader was talking nicely to him; she even whistled softly. Usually he likes that. I do. He should have calmed down. Not Shiloh.

Instructor started singing the Happy Song: "If you're happy and you know it...then your horse will surely show it." *Nice try.*

Mom came to the rescue. She brought him his pacifier. Can you believe that! A pacifier. Big Baby Shiloh just needed something to chew on. Well, it worked. We got on with the lesson.

Shiloh and Ace

Where all children are equal in the saddle

MOM TO THE RESCUE!

"Mom" is the Equine/Farm Director at Saddle Up! (Actually, there are two "moms," the director and the assistant, but although Hershey knows them as different people, both are just "Mom" to him.)

Mom knows things. Like which horses don't like to play basketball. (Don't think that is a joke. Saddle Up! riders frequently get to toss the ball from horseback into the basket. Most of the horses are fine with the ball going every which way. Some, like Gabby, are not.)

Mom knows which horses don't want more than one sidewalker and which are fine with having more people up close. Mom also knows when to use her MOM-VOICE to correct a horse and when to talk softly and be patient. Mom's job is to figure out what helps the horses be happy in *their* job. Even if that's a pacifier.

Shiloh, for whatever reason, is often insecure. He needs his buddy, especially Ace. He needs to know exactly what he's to do, and he needs attention. Perhaps because he was bottlefed as a foal, he gets "mouthy" and antsy when he's nervous. Mom affixed a chain with a large bolt to his sidepull (a bridle without a bit). It hangs right where Shiloh can reach it with his mouth when he needs to. The rest of the time it just clinks and chimes a soothing sound.

Thank you, Mom.

HERSHEY & THE MELTDOWN

Hershey, here.

Not every lesson is easy going. Every once in a while a rider will start crying or screaming. That's really scary! *What's wrong? What's wrong? Fix it! Fix it!*

Most times instructors can "fix it." For one thing, they have soothing voices. I feel better and so does the rider—usually, not always. Sometimes instructors have to figure out something different, quickly. They work hard to help every rider (and horse) have a good experience.

One day a meltdown happened even before my buddy, Harley, and I were out of the crossties. Harley's rider flat out refused to go near him, even though she had ridden him just the week before. *Made no sense to me—or Harley.* I could hear Instructor talking calmly to Rider, but she kept shaking her head, no. She wasn't going to budge!

Instructor turned to Harley's leader and said something. Leader took him away. *Sorry, Harley.*

In a few minutes Leader returned, this time with Webster. Instructor said, "You may not be ready to ride this week, but you can still be in the lesson." She handed Rider the lead rope. *What would she do?*

"Walk on, Webster." Off they went to the arena—the big girl and the tiny horse.

The first time I saw the minis, Webster and Sherman, I just knew they couldn't be good for much. Those horses could almost walk underneath me! Saddle Up! jobs are for real horses! (OK, for ponies too.) But minis!? Huh!

Those two little ones have been around for a while now, and they are just right for lots of things, including curing a meltdown. After two lessons leading Webster, Harley's rider was back in the saddle and smiling again.

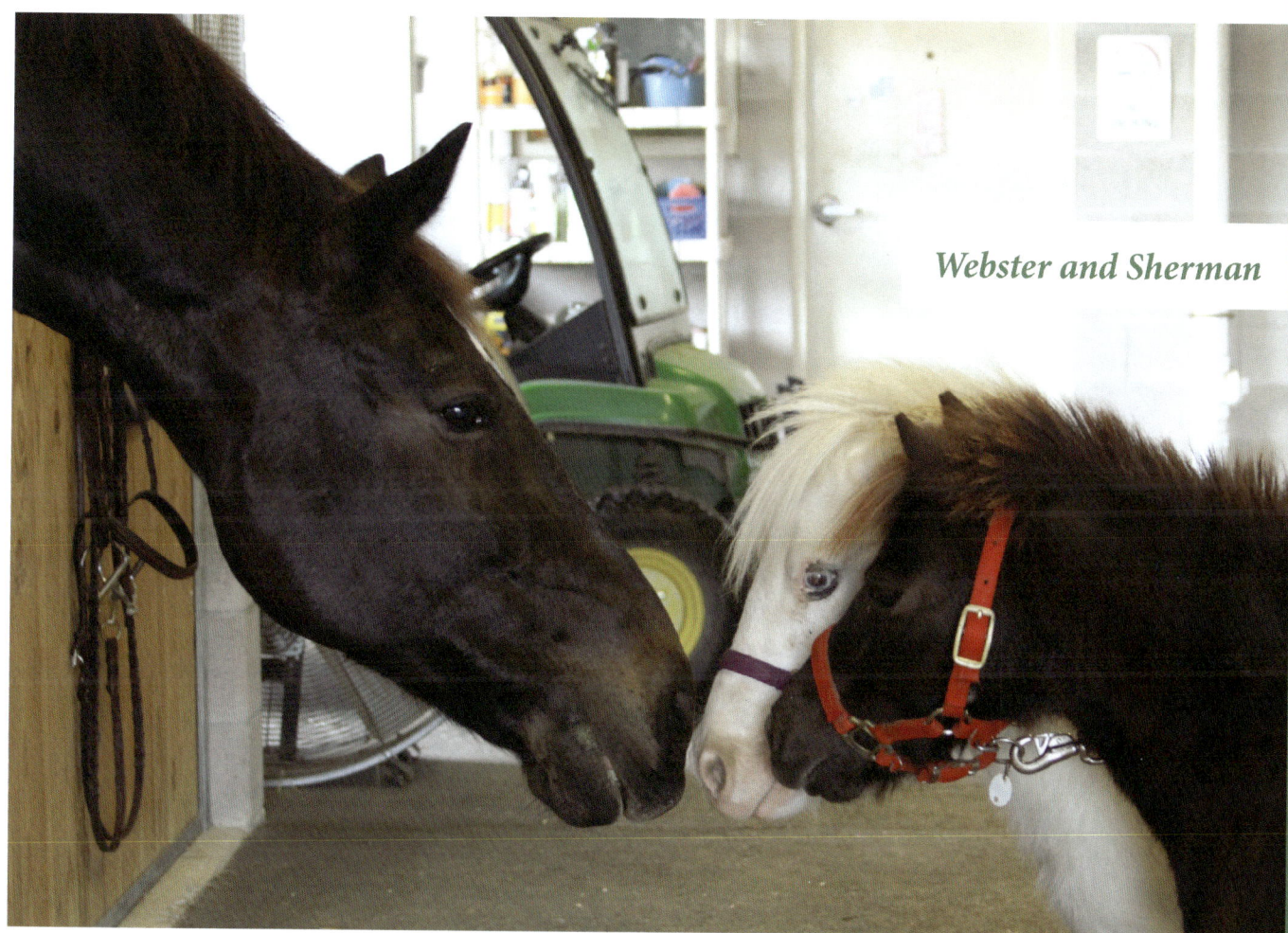

Webster and Sherman

NOT TOO LITTLE

Seeing a miniature horse the first time can be both a delight—they're so little and cute—and a puzzle. Unlike a horse or a pony, they can't be ridden. What can they do?

Minis are miniature! The smallest, according to *Guinness Book of World Records*, was only 17 inches (4.1 hands). Most are about twice that size, usually around 34 inches (8.2 hands). Webster is only 29 inches (7.1 hands). Compare that to Hershey, who is 14.2 hands. Then, of course, there's Pride! At 16.2 hands he's Saddle Up!'s tallest horse.

Minis are horses—not small ponies. Pony breeds have a somewhat different conformation (shape and build) from horses. Their legs are short and stout; their bodies have elongated torsos, and their neck is thicker than a horse's. A mini has the same build as a horse, just miniaturized.

Miniature horses have been around since the 1600's. Sometimes they were kept as pets, especially among royalty, and simply enjoyed for their gentle nature. But many were specifically bred for hard work. In the early 1800's, children as young as seven were forced to labor in coal mines for eleven to twelve hours a day. Finally, in 1842 England passed a law prohibiting the abuse. But society still needed coal. The industry turned to miniature horses, using them instead of children to pull carts out of the cramped spaces of the tunnels. That practice continued in some areas for nearly one hundred years.

Minis no longer work in mines or do other such hard labor, but some are trained as guide animals for people who are blind. Most minis today can be found on small farms enjoying life with their family or at special shows for miniature horses, delighting their fans with their beauty, versatility, and willing spirits.

Two very lucky minis have fans at Saddle Up! Yeah, Webster and Sherman!

A "Hand"

In the days before measuring tapes and rulers, people used the width of their hand to figure out how large their horses were. Today the standard is that a "hand" is four inches. Horses are measured from the top of their withers (the point where the neck joins the body) to the floor. Hershey is 58 inches tall, which translates into 14.2 hands (58 divided by 4 equals 14 with a remainder of 2 inches). At 16.2 hands Pride is 8 inches taller than Hershey! Webster, at 7.1 hands, is *half* the size of Hershey.

Not too little, just right

HERSHEY & THE SUPER SHOW

Hershey, here.

I love the SUPER Show at Saddle Up! Everybody is there. Everybody is excited! Even me. So much going on. Lots of noise. Lots of hurry-up-and-wait. I love it!

Not so with my buddy, Red. We were waiting in line (the hurry-up-and-wait part), and he just couldn't take it. His leader tried to calm him, but Red was really unhappy and started to act up. Finally, Mom showed up and took him away. *Red, you're missing the fun!*

At the SUPER Show I have several different riders. Some I don't know. But that's OK. *I know what to do.* My favorite thing is the obstacle course—it reminds me of trail riding. *I'm good at that!* I'm OK with doing the pattern-ride outside. I know it's in an arena, but, hey, it's outside! For all that, I can put up with the round-and-round ride inside, which is the last thing we do. It's super simple—mostly just walk on and whoa. Occasionally, a trot. *Easy!*

Sometimes Rider will be excited and happy. The next Rider might be a bit scared. I never know until I feel Rider in the saddle. *Not to worry, Rider! I'm here for you! It's the SUPER Show!*

Trail Obstacle Class

Dressage Pattern Ride

Round and Round Equitation Class

Where all children are equal in the saddle

EVERYONE IS A WINNER!

Super exciting is Saddle Up!'s Phenomenal Equestrian Riders (SUPER) Show. Parents, grandparents, brothers, and sisters come to watch their riders show off the skills they've been learning. The indoor and outdoor arenas have a special set up for the day.

Inside, volunteers scurry around, getting horses and riders ready. While outside, a church group set up grills and coolers and begin preparing to feed everyone.

The day is full with more than 60 riders participating. Most will ride in the three classes Hershey described: the obstacle course, the dressage (patterned riding) test, and the equitation class where, while the horses and riders go "round and round" in the arena, the judges are watching for each rider's correct position while mounted and his or her ability to effectively communicate to the horse what to do by using the aids—voice, reins, and legs—as the riders have learned in lessons.

Some participants also compete unmounted. In the showmanship class they walk with the horse in a specific pattern, displaying how well they and their horse work together. Others demonstrate their horse knowledge, identifying parts of the horse, horse colors, facial and leg markings, and the horses' body language.

All of the classes are a challenge, but Saddle Up! staff and volunteers make sure they are fun too!

Hershey doesn't get to see the rest of the action once his riders finish their classes. Riders, family, and volunteers go outside for the presentation of ribbons. Many of the riders leave with a ribbon to remember their accomplishments not only for the day of the SUPER Show, but also for the weeks of lessons leading up to it.

Just as in any other horse show, sometimes a rider won't place in the top six spots. But riders who don't earn a ribbon that day see something to aspire to, and proud families and volunteers make sure their riders know they are winners too. That's the Saddle Up! way.

Ice Cream Cones!

Occasionally—not often enough, according to Hershey—the riders in the Equestrian Club will make ice cream cone treats for their horses. Here's the recipe:

Mix together to a "scoop-able" consistency:

> Horse oats
> Bran
> Honey or molasses
> Crushed peppermint candy

Scoop the mix into a standard ice cream cone.

Serve to eager horses. (Watch out they don't nibble any fingers!)

Seen my new book?

Hershey, Here!
At Saddle Up!   Crys Zinkiewicz

Like horses?

You'll love Hershey!

and his stories about Saddle Up!

For horse-lovers of all ages!

Saddle Up! is Middle Tennessee's oldest and largest organization offering equine-assisted activities and therapies, serving children and youth with disabilities.

Proceeds from the book sales support Saddle Up!

To purchase the book or to find out about current Hershey events, visit hersheyhere.org

HERSHEY & "PONY CLUB"

Hershey, here.

Today is "Pony Club" day. I don't know why anyone would call it "Pony Club." All of us are horses—not ponies! Sometimes I hear Instructors say "Equestrian Club," but whatever it's called, I like it!

Five of us horses (no little ponies allowed!) each have our own girl or guy—no leader, no sidewalkers. *Nice change.* Girl comes to get me; she grooms me—and tries to find my tickle spot. She puts the saddle on me.

Girl's good about tightening the girth—that's really tricky: If she tightens too fast, I get upset. *(How would you like to be squeezed hard? Take it easy!)* If she doesn't tighten enough, the saddle is too loose and that's bad. One time before I came to Saddle Up! that happened, and the saddle ended up almost under my belly! I just stood really still. *(Somebody needs to do something—now!)* I don't worry about Girl. She is really careful to get the girth just right. And Instructor always checks too. Safety first!

Then we all ride. Girl is getting better and better. Most days we work in the arena on advanced riding skills or do challenge games like the Catalog Race and Ride a Buck. *Hey! I am not the one bucking!* Girl has to keep something called a "buck" between her leg and the saddle and not let it fall. My favorite challenge is the Cup of Water Trot. Sometimes I get splashed. *Feels good.*

Occasionally we go for a trail ride along the river. Instructors ride too. One day we had a big surprise. In the lead, Instructor's horse, Coffee, saw it first. *It wasn't supposed to be there!* Coffee spooked!

I tensed up. What?! What?! Should we run away?

Then I felt Girl—she wasn't scared. I relaxed. I trust Girl. We rode right past Coffee's "monster."

Seriously, Coffee, it's just a kayak in the woods—no big deal!

SADDLE UP!'S EQUESTRIAN CLUB

Throughout the year and during a week in the summer, five to six guys and girls (usually—but not exclusively—teenagers) participate in the Saddle Up! Equestrian Club. Hershey is right: Sometimes the riders refer to it as their "pony club," but horse people will often use the word "pony" as a term of affection. Even Muffin, one of the biggest horses at Saddle Up! has been called "my pony" by a rider who loves him.

These teens have been in lessons at Saddle Up! for several years and have progressed to the status of Independent Riders, but while they have learned much already, they are eager to know and do more. Central to the club is time with the horses and time in the saddle, but Equestrian Club members also watch the farrier care for the horses' feet and shoe them. They visit an equine vet to find out more about what horses need for good health. They go to a breeding farm where they see the newborns and watch the bigger foals play. They learn about trailering and practice loading their horses in a trailer. They even take a short ride on the Saddle Up! property in the back of the horse trailer, standing up themselves, to feel what the horses experience.

Club members would say they are learning about horses, but instructors know their charges are also learning responsibility, becoming more safety conscious, developing their self-confidence, and experiencing empathy. Both club members and instructors would agree—all of it is fun!

HERSHEY & THE CARDS

Hershey, here.

We were getting ready for "Pony Club" one day, but something felt wrong. Girl was not brushing me. She and the others were clustered around Instructor. *Oh, I see—somebody's missing! Where's my buddy Elvis?* He's supposed to be here too. His girl isn't here either.

Instructor sent two of the girls away in different directions. One came back with a container, brush, and paper. *That's odd.* Then the other came, leading Elvis to the crossties.

Girl forgot about me. Elvis got all the attention. *Hey! What's up with that? I'm still here.*

All the girls were with Elvis, talking to him, stroking him. All the girls—*except* his Girl.

My Girl picked up Elvis' front leg to pick out his hoof. *I would have let her have mine! But no, she's over there with Elvis!*

Then something even stranger happened. After Girl brushed out the hoof and pronounced it clean, another girl dipped a different kind of brush into the container and painted the bottom of Elvis's foot. One of the other girls placed the paper on the floor of the grooming area, and Girl carefully put Elvis's hoof down onto the paper. I have to say, Elvis was a good sport about all that—*but they better not try it with me.*

Then Girl asked Elvis to pick up his foot. *He's good—he did it first time.* Everyone was really excited, talking fast and waving the paper around. I caught a glimpse. It was Elvis's hoofprint. *What's the big deal?*

Instructor made some more marks on the paper and then each girl added some marks too. The paper disappeared, and finally we could get on with Pony Club.

The next week was pretty much the same, and the next too. Elvis got all the attention. But he did have to put up with the paint job on his hoof. *Better him than me!*

Finally, Elvis's girl came back. The other girls were all talking at once, happy to see her. So was Elvis. Maybe he was just glad not to have to make all those hoofprints. But when we were all together back in the arena, I saw Elvis's girl reach down and throw her arms around Elvis's neck. Elvis was licking and chewing—his Girl was back!

LEARNING TO CARE

Life can be hard at times. Saddle Up! kids know that fact all too well. Most of the time they and their families manage to find joy in the midst of it all and keep on, doing amazingly well despite the obstacles. However, sometimes life's handouts stack up and become too much to bear.

Being a teenager is plenty hard; being a teenager with a disability is infinitely harder. Some of Saddle Up!'s teens struggle with feeling invisible among their peers because of having a disability. For some, the disability, such as autism or an anxiety disorder, for example, pulls them inside themselves. Whatever the cause, the result is often isolation for the young person.

Saddle Up!'s Equestrian Club program works intentionally to create a safe environment where riders can forge bonds with the horses, who are nonjudgmental, and where friendships can blossom. As the members have found a common interest in being with the horses, participated in challenges that ask them to work as a team, and focused on what it means to care for a horse, they have also learned about caring for one another. Making the cards together to encourage their friend who was going through a particularly tough time was a step forward for all the members of the club.

Neither Hershey nor Elvis has any idea of how important they are to their riders, and especially to their girls in Equestrian Club. But for one young teen the cards "from Elvis" and the other girls were enough to help her along the way toward healing.

Where all children are equal in the saddle

HERSHEY & THE BUCKET LIST

Hershey, here.

My Pony Club buddies and I were in the crossties. I was all set just to relax and enjoy the brushing when I heard it: "bucket list." *Buckets! I know all about buckets. They have feed and treats in them! Bring on the buckets! Yeah!*

Well, that didn't happen. Grooming, tacking, riding... *OK, maybe when we're finished I'll get my treat.*

Riding was different that day. We did our usual warm up, but then we spent time in the Stop-and-Talk Spot in the center of the arena. We waited and watched.

First, Elvis and his girl rode to the rail and began trotting. Then Instructor yelled out, "Canter!" *That's different! Most of us at Saddle Up don't get to canter.* Elvis picked up his canter, but it didn't last very long. His girl didn't get the rhythm, so Elvis dropped back to a trot. Instructor was really happy though. She said nice things to Elvis's girl and stroked Elvis—and I heard it again: "bucket list." *Hmmm...*

Then Instructor did a really strange thing. She had Tucker's rider dismount, and she took off his saddle. *Are we done?* (The rest of us were still standing in the Stop-and-Talk Spot, watching.) *I guess not.* Instructor brought the small mounting block over to Tucker. *Hey! He doesn't have his saddle on!* Next thing I saw was Tucker's girl sitting on him bareback and then riding at a walk around the arena. *Hey! Can I be next? I love bareback riding!*

I was next, but I didn't get to go bareback. I had to do Figure 8's—one circle, then a second circle beside the first, but going in the opposite direction. *Good thing Pal showed me how to do those—Girl wasn't* quite sure. We finished our turn and went back to the Stop-and-Talk Spot. This time Instructor and Girl were stroking me. I heard it again: "bucket list." *OK, OK. I'm ready!*

The buckets did not appear! Girl did take the long way to the pasture and let me graze some. *OK, that was a treat, but it's not a bucket full.*

Next day and the day after and the day after I was surprised—we did Pony Club again. *That's different. OK with me, though.* Elvis and his girl got to try cantering again. I could tell she was getting better. Elvis could hold the canter longer each time. Tucker, lucky horse, took his rider bareback again, even doing a trot. Tucker told me later that his rider wasn't so scared or wobbly as on the first day. I agreed—she looked really happy. And Girl and I mastered those Figure 8's. "Good boy!" I heard her say.

Every day I heard it: "bucket list." Every day, no buckets.

The last day I'd given up. Arena time was over. Riders gave us an extra grooming, and then they all disappeared. Instructors waited with us. *Hmmm...*

We could hear the riders coming back, talking happily! Then there they were—with the buckets! *Yeah!*

Finally, we all got our bucket list wish.

Where all children are equal in the saddle

EMPOWERING!

As independent riders, Equestrian Club members are able to take on more challenges that increase their skills in riding, horse care knowledge, and teamwork. But they benefit in other ways too.

Coming weekly throughout the year, the riders develop special relationships—with their horse, their teammates, and their instructors. The two instructors have the privilege of watching the guys and girls blossom. They have many stories.

Muffin is one of the biggest horses at Saddle Up! At 16 hands, he can be intimidating to anyone having to look up at him—which is almost everyone! His girl was very scared at first. Indeed, she was unsure of herself in most every situation in her life. But week after week she climbed aboard despite her fear and rode. And week after week she and her big horse did better and better *together*.

The instructors saw changes in the teen. As her confidence in Muffin and her riding grew, she also became more outgoing in her relationships with the other members of the club. Her parents reported positive changes too at home and at school. After she graduated from the program at age 19, she even took the volunteer training and began helping out at Saddle Up!

The Bucket List story happened during the Equestrian Club's Summer Week. Throughout the year, instructors consistently encourage the members to make choices and to do things for themselves and for the team. That summer one of the riders brought the idea of the bucket list to the club members: Each of them would decide something they really wanted to do before the end of the week. For Tucker's rider it was to ride bareback; for Elvis's it was to canter. Hershey's Figure 8's were only part of his rider's bucket list. (But that's another story Hershey will tell.)

Feeling emotionally safe and encouraged, growing in confidence, meeting goals they set for themselves, the Equestrian Club riders find a new sense of their own power: *I can do it! We can do it!*

That's horsepower!

HERSHEY & THE MUSIC

Hershey, here.

I am not a dressage horse! The trail is my happy place. But since coming to Saddle Up!, I've learned a few things.

My friend, Coffee, is a dressage queen. She says dressage is mostly just doing the things any good horse knows, but doing them pretty- like dancing. I'm not sure what that is, but Coffee sure is pretty when she moves out.

At the SUPER Show we ride a simple dressage pattern. No big deal. But at Pony Club Summer Week, "dressage" seemed to be a *big* deal. The cones were out. Walk on to that one. Trot to a different one. Make a circle. Cross the arena to another cone. Do a Figure 8. Reverse at yet another cone and do it all again. Whoa in the middle of the arena.

At first I could feel uncertainty in Girl. *Well, if she doesn't know what to do, how can I?* But we did the pattern again—and again. *OK, she gets it. I get it.*

Then someone turned on the music. We must be going to play the Walk On and Whoa Game. I know that one! The music starts; we start. The music stops; we stop. *Funny, that's a game we play with the little riders.*

Girl asked me to walk on. *OK, listen for the whoa-place.* Then she asked me to trot. *No "whoa"?* We circled. We crossed the arena. *Still no "whoa."* Hmmm... We did our Figure 8—we're really good at that! Then it was reverse and do it all again. We rode to the middle and whoa'd. Then the music stopped. *Hmmm... Must not be the Walk On and Whoa Game.*

The next day I saw the cones out again. Again, the music played and we rode the pattern. I forgot about listening for the music to stop. I just listened for Girl's next cue. *I'm getting this!*

The next day the cones were out—and so were the grown-ups, leaning on the rail. *Hmmm...* Girl reached down and stroked me. "Relax, Hershey. Just move with the music. I'm here."

The music begins. I forget about the grown-ups. *This is my Girl—and we're dancing!*

DANCING PARTNERS

"Dressage" is a fancy word for a higher level of training, moving from the basics to world-class performance. In the sport of dressage, official rules dictate certain patterns to be mastered at specific levels before horse and rider can move up. Dressage is one of only three equine sports currently in the Olympics: dressage, jumping, and eventing.

Relatively few horses receive more than the basic training. Many go on to other disciplines in the world of horse sports: jumping, trail riding, eventing, roping, cutting, western pleasure, reining, and polo, to name just a few. In each, the key to joy both in riding and in watching is the partnership between the horse and rider.

And in dressage, whether in the Olympics or at Saddle Up!, that partnership truly looks like dancing.

Two of the girls in the Equestrian Club, as part of their bucket list for the week, created their own patterns, chose their own music, and rode their Freestyle-With-Music dressage test. Elvis' rider included a canter in hers, and Hershey's "dance" had two perfect Figure 8's!

Everyone—the riders, the other members of the Equestrian Club, the instructors, and the "grown-ups" who had gathered to watch—all were thrilled with the performance.

And Hershey was licking and chewing. *Good job, partner!*

Bucket List completed!

Where all children are equal in the saddle

Equine Assisted Learning

HERSHEY & THE HERD OF KIDS

Hershey, here.

I was in the paddock where I usually graze until Leader comes to get me for a lesson. The minis, Sherman and Webster, were grazing there too. So were the ponies, Dumpling and Lucy, and my big buddy, Harley. Then we heard it!

Our heads shot up! Our ears were on high alert! We turned to stare at the barn! Something was coming!

Oh, my... It's a herd... a herd of kids!

I like the kids of Saddle Up! I really do. But they don't come all together like that. *What's going on?* They kept coming. They were noisy and busy. They were moving every which way, but coming toward us!

I glanced at *my* herd. Every one of us was ready to run from this fearful thing! But as the kids and volunteers came closer, I heard Instructor say, "Watch their ears. The horses are talking to you." *You bet I'm talking— and I have plenty to say!*

Harley on high alert

Suddenly the kids quieted down. *OK, that's better.*

That herd stayed outside my herd's paddock. *Maybe we'd be OK after all.* Dumpling dropped his head and started eating again. So did Webster. Lucy swished her tail, turned, and trotted to the far side of the paddock to watch. Sherman moved closer to Webster but kept his head up. *Those two minis watch out for each other.*

Instructor said something, and her herd stepped up to the fence. My neck stiffened; my ears pointed. *Just when I was starting to relax, they come at us again!*

Instructor continued talking. Then she opened the gate, calmly came inside, and closed it. *Whew! It's just her. I know her. She's OK.* She walked toward me. My ears came forward. *What she's doing? This is interesting.* She reached up and stroked my neck and said, "Hershey, these are the EAL students. They're learning to read your ears."

Instructor let one student and volunteer at a time come into the paddock. She asked each student to say which one of us was relaxed. Each student had to have a right answer before coming closer.

The students were good. All of us got petted and talked to—all of us except Lucy. Her ears still said, "Leave me alone!" Smart kids. They learned the first lesson that day.

TALKING EARS

During the school year Saddle Up!'s Equine Assisted Learning (EAL) program serves almost all of the 60+ students of a nearby private school that focuses on educating children and youth who learn differently. They each come in smaller groups to Saddle Up! three times for encounters with their new teachers—the horses.

When students first arrive, they are understandably excited and do not know what to expect as they take in the unfamiliar sights and sounds surrounding them at the farm. They meet their instructor and the volunteers (each student will have one), get fitted for their helmet (a required safety rule for being around the horses), and as they walk through the barn, begin a journey that will change their lives.

They come out of the barn noisy and distracted. Then... they see the horses. The students quiet down and focus. They are ready to learn.

The first EAL lesson is how to "read" the horses' body language. Are they comfortable and relaxed? Are they nervous and on the lookout for danger? (Horses are prey animals. Fleeing/flight is a survival skill.) Are they interested? Listening? Or seemingly angry? (Fight is their second survival skill.) Are they calm and resting, perhaps even dozing? (Horses can sleep standing up.) The horses' ears give the answers.

As the students learn to read the horses' ears and body language (including the stiffening of the neck in high alert and the swishing of the tail in annoyance), they work on transferring what they have seen with the horses to learning to read the body language of people. They go a step further in each lesson to talk about how being attentive to body-language cues can help them at school and in other social situations.

Hershey, Lucy, Dumpling, and the others have no idea that they are the teachers; but as one student declared, "Horses always tell you what they are thinking. They are so honest."

Where all children are equal in the saddle

HERSHEY & THE HOOF PICKS

Hershey, here.

My buddies, Pedro and Harley, and I are in the crossties. Instructor passes out hoof picks to the EAL students and points toward us.

One student steps right out and goes straight to Pedro. Pedro knows about hoof picks—we all do. Pedro is good about having his hooves picked—not all of us are. Student reaches down to Pedro's hoof, and of course Pedro picks it up for him. But Student doesn't know what to do next. He drops the hoof pick and then he drops Pedro's hoof! *Hey! Be careful—don't hurt my buddy!* Student goes back to the group. Talking. More talking. Then doing something—I can't see what.

Student comes back to Pedro. This time he's not so fast—he's more careful. This time when Pedro picks up his hoof, Student puts a hand under it to help Pedro out. This time Student holds on to both the hoof and the hoof pick. This time he works at picking the dirt out of the hoof. It takes several tries, but when he puts Pedro's hoof down, gently this time, it is clean. And Student is happy.

Instructor nudges another student toward Harley, but Student turns back. "I'm afraid," I heard her say. *Well, Harley is big—bigger than me—but he's as good as little Pedro about picking up his feet.* Instructor and Student talk. Talk some more.

Then Student takes a few steps toward Harley... and stops again. Harley lowers his head, ears forward, and looks at her. *I won't hurt you. You can do it.* Student reaches out and strokes his shoulder. Pretty soon Harley has clean feet too. And Student is happy.

Uh oh... my turn. I'm OK with having three of my hooves cleaned, but not that first one. Student is trying, but I just won't give him my foot. I can feel him getting angry. He goes back to the group. Talking. More talking. *Hmmm...*

Student comes back. This time he strokes me. Whew! He's not angry now. Student walks past my hard-to-do foot to the next one. I'm OK with that one. I pick it up when he asks. He moves to my other front foot and then to the other hind foot. No problem. Then Student comes back to the first foot and asks. *Hmmm... OK, I'll do it for you.* I pick up my foot this time. And Student is happy.

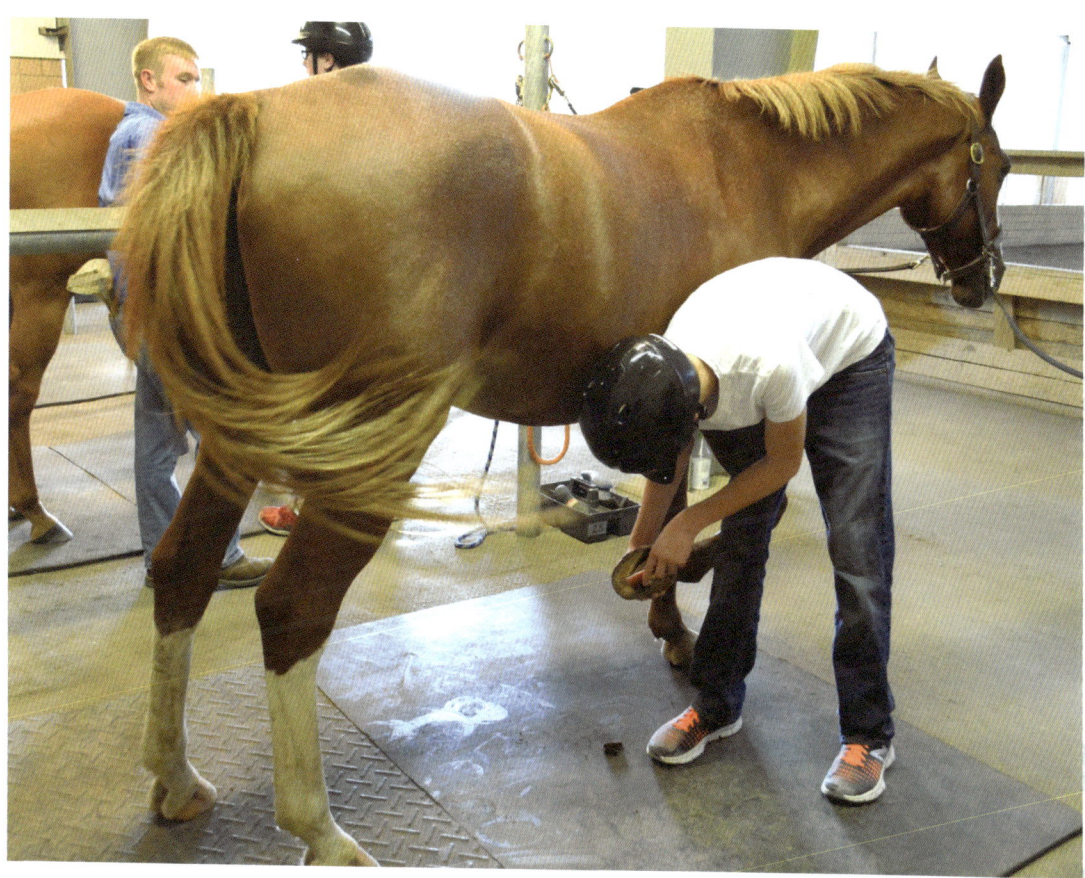

Where all children are equal in the saddle

MAKING GOOD DECISIONS

Few people would connect picking the dirt out of a horse's hoof with the skill of making good decisions—unless they knew about EAL at Saddle Up! The lesson, which is specifically for middle-school and high-school students enrolled in the program, takes them beyond the task into a life-learning: how to face something new—even if it is daunting—and make it safe and do-able.

Hershey witnessed some of the aha moments.

Pedro's student, who rushed in, discovered he would be better served to observe and be thoughtful before acting. He was affirmed that asking for help for what he didn't know was not a weakness but a smart idea. He made a mistake, but he learned he was not a failure.

Harley's student, whose fear threatened to send her to the sidelines of life, discovered the importance of that first EAL lesson on reading body language. She was able to recognize and acknowledge what her own body was telling her. Then the instructor helped her explore options for what to do. With the encouragement of the instructor and her friends—and the gentle body language of her big-hearted Harley—she could observe the situation and judge it to be safe. She found the courage to try. She learned she could manage the risk, try something new, and have fun doing it.

Hershey's student got a bit more "equine assistance" than expected. But he stepped back, away from his frustration and anger, to observe, to read the horse, and to realize Hershey was not "out to get him" or to make him "look like a fool." Instead of "blowing up" or quitting, he explored the options he had and thoughtfully came up with a different approach. He learned he could be a problem-solver.

Thinking before doing, reading the situation and the feelings, exploring options, and managing risks are skills that the EAL students will hold onto long after they have put down their hoof picks.

HERSHEY & THE BALL GAME

Hershey, here.

My buddies, Harley, Dumpling, Pedro, Webster, Sherman, and I were grazing in the paddock, waiting for the next Summer Fun activity. *Hey! I think they're coming.* One little kid and his volunteer walked toward us, carrying cones. *Hmmm...* They went into the paddock beside us and set them up. *That's different—cones are for the arena, not outside.*

Then my Little Kid and the others came. This time with lead ropes. They were coming to get us. *OK!* But no, Little Kid went right past me and over to Dumpling. *Hey! I'm here. Don't forget me.* Little Kid and another little kid hooked their lead ropes to Dumpling. *Hey! Let him have Dumpling. You can have me.*

But no, one on each side, the little kids led Dumpling out—right past me—into the other paddock. Webster and Sherman got to go too, but Pedro, Harley, and I were left behind just to watch.

Dumpling, Webster, and Sherman, with a little kid on each side, were all standing behind one of the cones. Volunteers moved to the other cones. Instructor was at the one in the middle. All quiet.

Then shrieking and yelling erupted!

Team Sherman

Where all children are equal in the saddle

Instructor had rolled a ball toward Dumpling. His little kid kicked the ball and ran, urging Dumpling and the other little kid toward the next cone. Everyone was yelling, "Go! Go! Yeah, Dumpling! You can make second base!"

Then suddenly, Instructor used her mom-voice: WHOA! Everything stopped. Dumpling and his little kids halted at the second cone. No one was talking.

Webster and his little kids now faced Instructor. Everybody was tense. My ears were straight up! Something was about to happen. The ball! The ball! Kicked! Webster and his little kids running. Dumpling too. Next cone. Next cone.

WHOA! Webster stopped. Laughter and chatter didn't. *What's happening? What's happening?*

"Ready?" Instructor called. All quiet again. Again, the ball rolled. This time Sherman kicked it! *Yeah, Sherman!* More running! More laughing! This time no one seemed to hear the "whoa."

Hey! I want to play too.

Team Webster

SUMMER FUN AT SADDLE UP!

Equine Assisted Learning (EAL) takes a different turn in the summer. During the school year, the program serves students from the nearby school, but in the summer EAL is more like a week-long summer day camp and open to all the Saddle Up! participants. As with the school-year program the lessons are unmounted, but with more time available the activities are many and varied. Two of the weeks are for younger children; two are for older ones.

One of the themes of the week is teamwork—being partners with the horse and with the other participants. The set up for the Kick-the-Ball Game is similar to a baseball diamond with a pitcher's mound, three bases, and home—each marked with a cone. Teams of two kids (with one of the smaller equines) have to decide who will be the kicker, and then they have to work together to give their horse or pony clear direction as to where to go as they run to each base and, of course, to stop when they hear the "whoa."

Perfection is not the goal. Whether one child heads in one direction and the other in a different one (with or without the pony) or the ball bounces off a hoof instead of a foot doesn't really matter. Everyone has fun. Everyone learns through the experiences and the discussions. Everyone gets to be part of a team (some for the very first time). Everyone is a winner.

The last day of the Summer Fun week focuses on what makes each one special. The activities of the day culminate in a parade, which the families come to see. Each child has decorated his or her horse with paint, stickers, and ribbons, making all the horses special for the day too.

One at a time the kids lead their horse through an obstacle course, showing their skills in showmanship. At the end, they step into the "spotlight," a square marked by poles on the ground. Here they stop to face the audience. They first tell something about what makes their horse special, then what makes one of the other members of their team special, and finally something that is special about themselves. Along with appreciation for others, the Summer Fun participants gain a new appreciation for themselves. That is the prize each one takes home!

Where all children are equal in the saddle

Summer Fun!

The Spotlight!

Therapy Services

HERSHEY & THE VERY LITTLE PATIENT

Hershey, here.

One day Instructor—not Leader—came to get me. Then, instead of a saddle, I got a bareback pad with a ring on each side. She put the bridle on and the bit in my mouth, but the bridle had no reins. *OK... something's going on here.*

Then a new person, Therapist, came. She stroked my neck and talked to me. She checked the girth on the bareback pad. Then she attached long lines—really long lines—to my bridle and ran them through the rings on the bareback pad. *This is definitely different!*

Instructor gathered up the long lines and walked beside me into the arena. Therapist stood to the side giving *instructions* to Instructor. *Confusing.* But then Therapist began saying "Handler" instead of "Instructor." *Things are changing!*

Handler straightened out the long lines and stepped behind me. "Walk on, Hershey, walk on." *Finally, something makes sense again.* I walked forward. I felt the tug on my bit and I turned. Another tug and I slowed down. *Oh, I see. It's not that much different, after all.*

That day and the next day and the next day we worked in the arena. I did circles, reverses, serpentines, and my favorite, Figure 8's, on the long line. I could tell when Handler wanted me to speed up or slow down, go straight or turn. *No problem. I've got this!*

Then comes Patient. I look at her. She looks at me. She stamps her foot and says, "No!" *Awww...*

Well, I am big. She is very little.

Therapist finally convinces her to try. Patient is on my back, sort of.

Mostly, she's just leaning over holding on to Therapist. I can feel her fear. We walk on. I go real easy.

Another week and Patient is back. Therapist takes her hand to help her touch me. I hold very still. We ride again. Patient is still clinging to Therapist, mostly, but she does try some of the movements. I shift my weight to help her balance. When we are done, Patient pets me. Ahhh...

The next week, Patient comes *right up to me!* I'm still big, but today she's not so very little anymore. We ride again.

Where all children are equal in the saddle

WALK LIKE ME

Horses bring to a therapy session their whole, wonderful selves, but their special gift is the way they walk. Rhythmical, repetitive, and multidimensional (able to move front to back, to shift side to side, and to rotate, turning on one leg and then the other), the horse's walk is like a human's—just with four legs.

For children with limited or no ability to walk or sit independently, simply being on a moving horse gives their bodies physical input. Weak muscles nevertheless grow stronger because the horse's movement provides the needed stimulus. Especially for the younger children, whose brains are still developing rapidly, the simulation of natural walking also strengthens the brain-body connection and leads to a better outcome in the long term. At Saddle Up! patients can begin the Therapy Services program as young as age two.

The approach is not teaching riding skills as it is in the Recreational Therapeutic Riding program; rather it is to help the children develop daily living skills, ones they will need after they are off the horse: being able to sit independently, to increase mobility, to improve posture and balance, to use their hands to feed and dress themselves. As the children grow in these skills, they are better able to play and to participate with their peers, which is ultimately the "work" of childhood. A few of the patients "graduate" and are able to participate in the Therapeutic Riding program.

In the Saddle Up! Therapy Services program "handlers" are certified instructors. Volunteers can assist after special training. They become "supporters" rather than side-walkers.

The therapists know the needs of each child and work with the Equine/Farm Director to carefully match the horse or pony to help the individual. In the sessions the therapist will assist patients, supporting them but also moving them into various positions, riding backward or sideways, kneeling, or lying down—front, back, or across the body of the horse, for example. These changes stimulate different muscles. It's a whole-body workout!

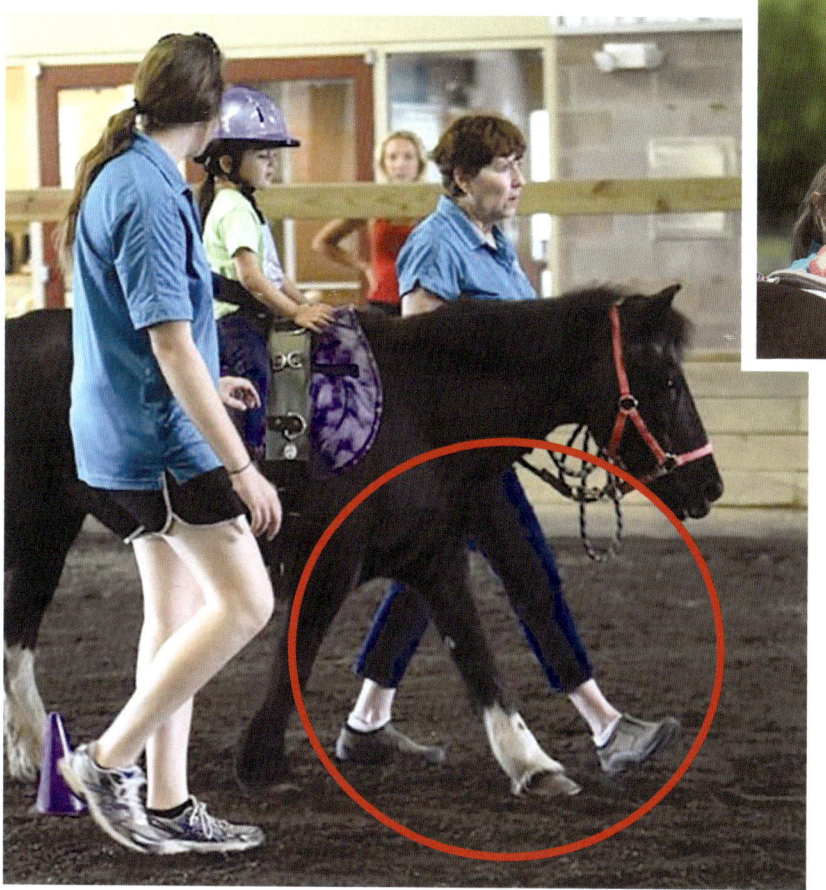

The horses chosen for the therapy sessions, like Hershey, need to be especially accepting of the frequent shifts in the child's position by the therapist. But they also go through extra training before they can begin. The horses must show proficiency in a series of maneuvers, including circles, serpentines, Figure 8's, reverses across the diagonal of the arena, shortening and lengthening stride, and staying straight in the long lines, all of which effectively challenge and strengthen the patient's body.

Hershey's "very little" Patient got "bigger" in so many different ways—Hershey has no idea! He was just doing his job, walking on. And being Hershey.

Where all children are equal in the saddle

82.

HERSHEY & THE CHIMES

Hershey, here.

Most of the time I'm pretty OK with surprises—not always, of course. But I'm a trail horse—I like adventures. *Good thing!*

Coming and going on my way to the barn or my pasture, I could see something happening in the field. Finally, Pal and I were headed there. I could check it out. (Pal is good about letting me look at strange things. A horse does have to be on the look out for predators, you know.)

We went first to bridge. *Up an over—no problem.* Then Pal stopped me at the boxes. She wanted me to stand still while she opened the doors. *OK.* Then she banged the door shut! *I fooled her—I didn't even flinch!*

Next stop was the toss spot. She threw beanbags at the holes—and missed. *Pal, you are not very good at this game.* We moved on.

When we got close to the noodles that first time, I was not happy. Horses know to avoid things that can jump down on their back. These were moving back and forth, going round and round too. I just knew they'd be trouble. But Pal didn't make me go under them. She turned me to the side so I could see them. I looked, and then I stuck my nose out to investigate. She kept telling me they were no big deal. *OK, Pal, if you say so.* We went through them. She was right. No big deal.

The swinging ball was high up too. But, hey, I play basketball with riders in the arena. I'm used to balls that fly past my head.

One more thing. Tubes hanging down. *Hmmm...* Before Pal could stop me, I grabbed one with my teeth. It was *not* a treat! I let it go! And surprise—I heard music!

This place is fun!

Where all children are equal in the saddle

THE FUN FACTOR

Hershey just described his introduction to the Sensory Field at Saddle Up! Built as an Eagle Scout project, the field is a great addition to both the Therapeutic Riding and the Therapy Services programs. The different stations (the bridge, the touch boxes, the beanbag toss into various shapes and colors, the noodle curtain, swinging ball, and Hershey's chimes) provide both sensory input and fun!

Fun is definitely good therapy!

All of the children who come for therapeutic riding or who participate in the therapy services have had multiple visits to doctors, hospitals, therapists, and clinics. Many, starting as infants. Some days having to go again is just too much, and the child "melts down." But not so with visits to Saddle Up! The children simply don't think of going there as "therapy"—it's just fun!

Being outside in the Sensory Field adds to the fun.

A child goes through the curtain of noodles and laughs! He turns, looking for mom to make sure she saw him. He's having fun, but he's also rotating—using those muscles, with the horse's help.

The child with sensory-integration issues hears the chimes, feels the noodles touch him, reaches into the box where he cannot see but can touch the "treasure" inside. It's fun!

The girl transfers from her wheelchair to her horse. No longer is she a passenger in a one-dimensional vehicle. On horseback her body is engaged in multiple dimensions, including the fun factor.

The professional therapists at Saddle Up! also have practices in hospital and clinical settings, sometimes seeing the same children in their office and at Saddle Up! Consistently, the therapists—and parents—see the patients making progress toward their individualized goals, often even faster with the horses.

Something to celebrate! *Ring those chimes, Hershey!*

Where all children are equal in the saddle 85.

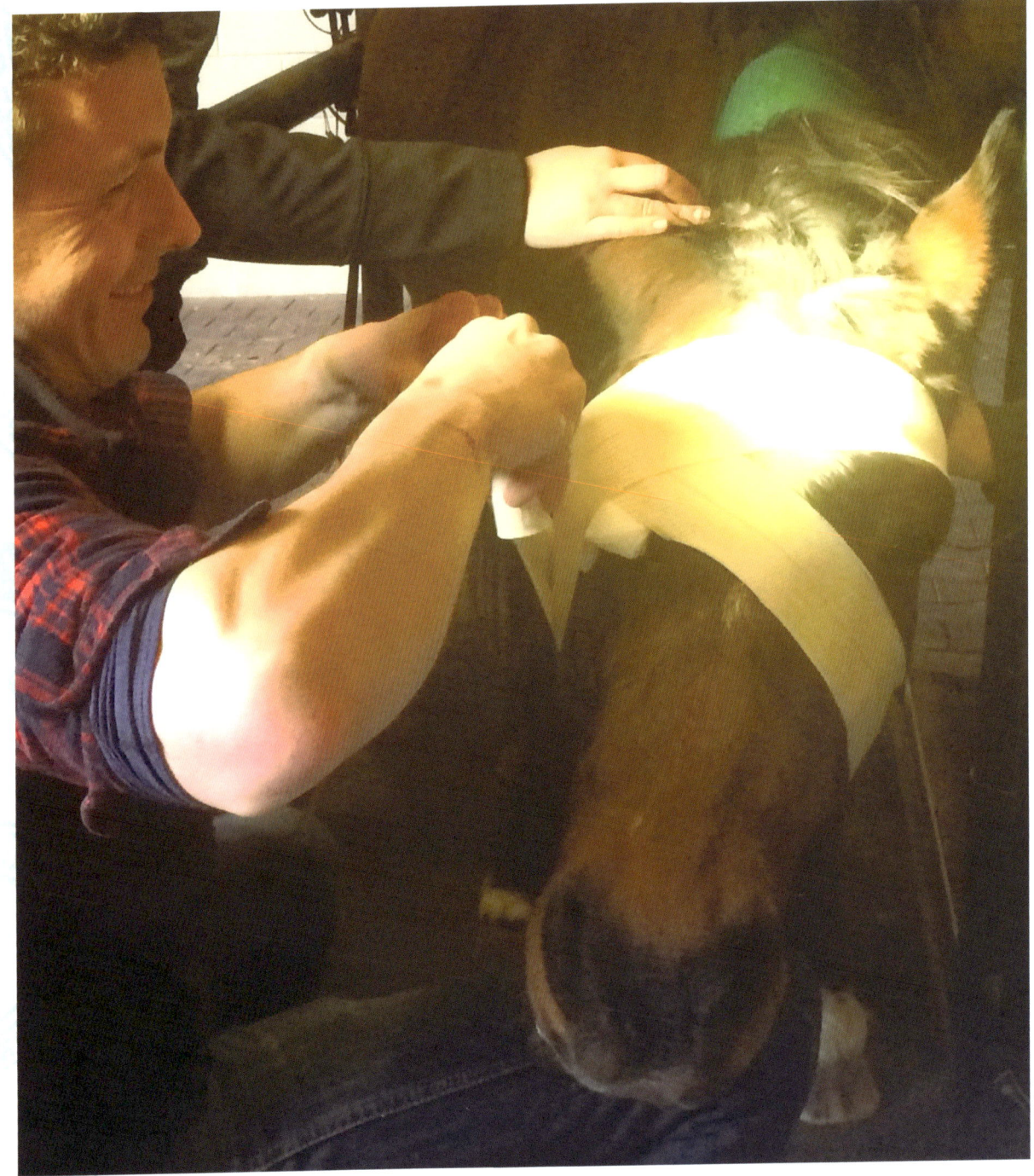

86.

SECOND-CHANCE LANCE

"What's wrong with him?" "Will he be OK?"

For weeks the children came to visit Lance in his stall. They forgot their own issues in their concern for him.

Lance was glad to see them. But seeing them was the problem. Lance's head was bandaged, covering up the empty socket where his eye used to be—before the surgery.

The Moms and the vet had done everything they could, but the disease was damaging the eye irreparably. For Lance's sake, the eye had to go.

Would he be OK? Would he ever be able to be a therapy horse again? The months of healing made the questions even bigger. Losing an eye can make an animal fearful, robbing it of energy and focus, of dignity. Would that happen to Lance?

With a shake of his head, Lance declared, "No!" Finally out of the stall, the bandage gone, Lance was on his own—sort of. In the paddock Coffee was there on his blind side. He could hear her. Fortunately, hearing is a horse's strongest sense, rather than seeing. Lance could walk with Coffee. Each day he figured out more how to get around safely, then easily.

The Moms, the therapists, the handlers agreed, "Let's give Lance a second chance!"

Lance had to go through two evaluations. The day of the first test presented an unexpected challenge. A Bobcat-tractor was working in the arena. The unusual and loud noise didn't faze Lance. So the evaluation team took him to the Sensory Field instead. He did every test there perfectly, even when asked to cross the bridge sideways, which he had never done before. A different day, when the Bobcat wasn't working, Lance also performed flawlessly in the arena.

Second-chance Lance is now back in the Therapy Services program, assisting and inspiring patients—his kids.

When the children who come to Saddle Up! see Lance for the first time, they often ask,

"What's wrong with him?"
"He has a disability."
"Will he be OK?"
"He's just fine—
and so are you!"

Where all children are equal in the saddle

PADDOCK, PASTURE, AND TINY SPACE

Paddock, pasture, and the Tiny Space are all enclosed spaces where horses can move about freely and graze. What distinguish the three are size, location, and purpose.

Pastures are larger; paddocks are smaller. The Tiny Space is, well, tiny—from a horse's perspective. It's about three times the size of one of the large box stalls in the Saddle Up! barn.

Paddocks are closer to the center of people action, whatever that is. At Saddle Up! the horses are moved from their pastures to the paddocks before lessons, so they can be close to the barn to minimize the time needed to bring a horse in for a lesson. After their lessons are done for the day, the horses are taken back to their pasture—like going home for supper after a good day's work.

The Tiny Space is a helpful enclosure for allowing a recovering horse limited movement so that it can heal. At Saddle Up! the area is in the corner of the nearest pasture so the Moms can keep a close eye on the patient and the horse or pony can be outside and near the other horses. Loving care, sunshine, and friends! What everyone—horse (and human)—needs!

Hershey's Herd

HERSHEY & THE NEW ARRIVAL

Hershey, here.

The first time I saw her I knew I had to tell her. Her feet stunk. *Poor thing.*

Every day I would see her—sometimes more than once. But she was either in her stall or in the Tiny Space. Someone was always leading me past her. I couldn't stop to tell her. She looked *awful*.

I noticed right away she had extra hay. The Moms were spending a lot of time with her, brushing her, stroking her, talking to her, lovin' on her—giving her *treats!* I had to tell her. This treatment is not going to last!

At least, her feet didn't stink anymore.

I had to tell her, but how?

Lacy, that's her name. I found out from my buddy Pride, who found out from Coffee, who was in the pasture next to the Tiny Space. I tried to tell Pride for him to tell Coffee for her to tell Lacy, but I don't think that happened. Maybe they didn't believe me. They both came to Saddle Up! after I did. They didn't really know.

Then one day, as I was led past, I noticed Lacy was looking better—not so thin. Extra hay, extra treats—*I knew it!*

One day Lacy was missing! She wasn't in her stall—I looked. She wasn't in the Tiny Space either. *Where is she? I have to tell her.*

Then I saw her. She was finally out of the Tiny Space and in the pasture next to mine. If I could just get her attention...

I would tell her. I hung out at the fence. I watched her. She moved so slowly. I called to her.

Lacy! Lacy, it's Hershey, here. Come closer. I have something to tell you.

Not that first day, but finally she came. Now I could tell her myself—forget Pride and Coffee!

I told Lacy my story. When I first came to Saddle Up!, like Lacy, I was hungry and hurting. My feet didn't stink, but my foot was cut open and festering. I hadn't had a good meal in many, many days. My coat was awful. I wasn't the strong, beautiful horse that I am today. I had to tell her so she would know that at Saddle Up! she too would someday soon be the healthy, beautiful horse she deserved to be.

We spent lots of hours near each other in our two pastures. Then she was gone more and more. But each time she came back happy. She was finally working again; she'd been in the arena, learning new things. Soon she was doing a lesson and then a few more. The Moms were happy.

Then Lacy told me she had a pal too. I was happy. Yesterday our pals took us out for a treat—a trail ride. Together! I was showing off a bit. She was truly beautiful and healthy.

Lacy headbutted me. "Hershey, I love Saddle Up!"

Told you so!

You were right, Hershey!
— Lacy

Where all children are equal in the saddle

Lacy's now healthy, beautiful coat

THE HEART OF THE MATTER

Hershey wasn't the only one to do a double take when Lacy first arrived at Saddle Up! She looked so different from the rest of the herd. Her ribs were showing—she was terribly underweight. Her coat was dull and brittle. And yes, her feet stunk. She had a severe case of thrush, an infection that rots away the sole of the foot. It's a disease that comes from neglect and poor care, which stinks!

Most of Saddle Up!'s horses come in good shape. Young riders outgrow their ponies or lose interest or students go off to college and career, and the families know Saddle Up! will take good care of their beloved friends. Or the owner's life changes—a growing family, a divorce, a move for a job, a job loss, ill health. Many different circumstances can precipitate a need to find a new home for a horse. Most people who donate horses to Saddle Up! have taken good care of their horses, but occasionally that is not the case.

Lacy's owner became very ill and was hospitalized for months. She had no one except some kind neighbors to take care of the horses. Unfortunately, the neighbors did not know anything about caring for horses. Lacy and the others in her herd suffered.

When the offer to donate two of the horses came, Saddle Up!'s Equine/Farm Manager and Assistant (the Moms) went to try them out. Both horses were in poor condition; but despite her sore feet, her hunger, and her weakened state, Lacy willingly did everything Mom asked of her. Not so with the other horse.

The mission of Saddle Up! is not to rescue horses, as much as that is needed. The Equine/Farm Director and Assistant are charged with finding the *right* horses for the job of serving the children and teens who are the mission of Saddle Up! Sometimes that means looking beyond the effects of being hungry and hurting to see the heart of the horse. That was true for Lacy—and for Hershey.

Where all children are equal in the saddle

HERSHEY & THE KISS

Hershey, here.

I love playing with Mom.

When it's cold out (but not too cold), my favorite game is Mess Up My Blanket. Mom puts it on straight at the end of the day, and I make sure it's not straight anymore when she comes to get me in the morning. A few of my buddies play, but Mom says I'm the best at the game.

When the weather changes and the flies come, most all of us, except Lucy (she has her own fan), play the Hide the Fly Mask game. When Mom comes to the pasture, she never knows who will have gotten off the fly mask or where it's hidden. We pretend we're grazing, but we like watching her hunt. I'm really good at that game too, but Harley's the best. One day he pawed a hole and put the fly mask in it. Mom didn't find it for days. *Good one, Harley!*

Mom, you're fun to play with!

But when I hurt, I really love Mom. She makes the hurt go away.

My foot—the one that was hurt when I first came to Saddle Up!, the one I hate to pick up for anyone to clean—that foot is the one Mom has to fix most often. Usually, with the Silver Slipper.

At first, I hated the Silver Slipper. I'd do my best to pull away. But Mom was strong. She got the wrap on. Finally, I figured out that all her fussing with taping the Silver Slipper on my foot was helping me feel better.

One day I was in the crossties with my hurt foot again. Mom was wrapping it again and talking to me in her "feel better, Hershey" voice. I just had to do it...

I leaned down and "whuffled" in her ear. She turned to look at me, and I planted a big ol' Hershey kiss on her!

I love you, Mom!

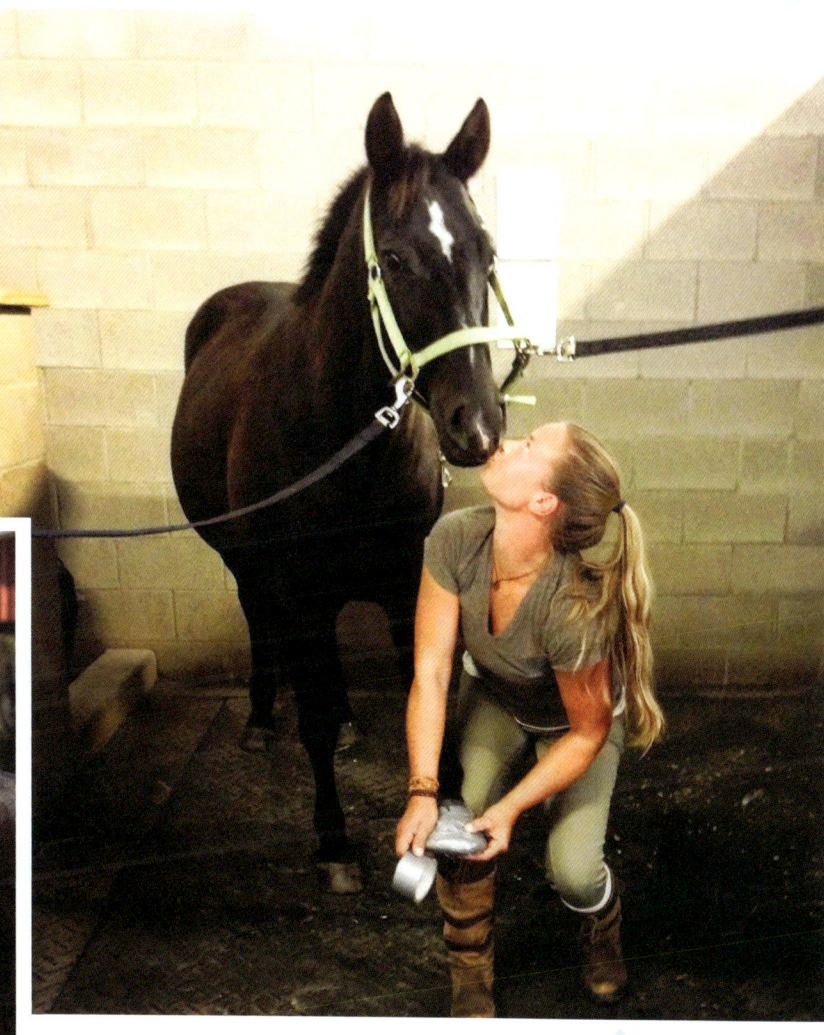

Let's play the Fly Mask game!

Where all children are equal in the saddle

SILVER SLIPPERS AND SO MUCH MORE

The Equine/Farm Director and Assistant (the Moms) have a big, 24/7 job caring for Saddle Up!'s herd of twenty-four, plus the three barn cats.

Sure, they have good volunteer helpers: leaders who groom and tack the horses; pony pals who assist with conditioning, training, and pampering their assigned horse; feeders who faithfully come every day morning and night; and stablehands who keep stalls and the rest of the barn clean, plus help out in various other ways.

They also have good professional help when needed: the farrier (horse shoer), the vet, the horse masseuse. Their other partner is Saddle Up!'s full-time Farm Manager, who cares for the pastures, fences, trails, arenas, equipment, barns, and other facilities of the 34-acre property.

But the Director and Assistant are truly "Mom" to the horses. They work with the scheduling of the sessions to make sure the horses have a good work/rest balance each week. They seek out and train new horses that will be a good fit for the job at Saddle Up!, and they diligently look for new homes for horses that are ready to retire.

They get to know each horse as an individual, learning each one's strengths and "issues" (like hating basketball or needing a pacifier occasionally). And they find ways to use the strengths and to avoid potential problems. They communicate that information to the instructors and volunteers so that everyone is working on the same team.

That knowledge of the horses also means the Moms can do a last-minute swap in a lesson if the assigned horse is lame or agitated for some reason and consequently unusable. They make sure every rider has a horse when lesson time comes.

The Moms are also "nurses" to the horses. Lameness, soreness, a cut, a fungus—Moms to the rescue! Whether first-aid, critical care, or chronic day-in-day-out care over time, the Moms deliver. Sometimes in creative ways. Like wrapping an injured hoof in duct tape. The Silver Slipper is the preferred Band-aid of the horse world.

The horses can count on the Moms to care for them no matter what. In 2010 the sky poured out 13.5 inches of water in two days. The Saddle Up! property was one of more than 11,000 that suffered from the resulting Great Flood. But Mom was there moving the horses out of harm's way. In 2015 a solid inch of ice covered the roads to and from Saddle Up! No one could get to the horses. But Mom was already there. She and her family stayed all night and day for three days, handling all the care of all the herd, keeping them sheltered and safe, feeding them, and making sure the water sources were not frozen too.

No wonder Hershey loves his Mom—even when he's hiding his fly mask!

Vet on hand . . . or foot

Where all children are equal in the saddle

HERSHEY & THE GOOD-BYES

Hershey, here.

I used to like seeing the horse trailer come out. But that was when I was a trail horse. Man and I were going places! We always came back after our adventures. But then the trailer took me to Saddle Up! and I didn't go back.

Sometimes the trailer means fun ahead. Sometimes it means good-bye.

I've watched Beau and Tommy and J.C. and Gretel step willingly into the trailer and never come back. I wanted to warn them, but I didn't have a chance.

And maybe, just maybe, they were off to adventures. Lacy and Tex did go for a trail ride with the Moms one day. They came back. Shiloh and Ace went to a different arena one time with their riders. They came back.

But not Beau or Tommy or J.C. or Gretel.

Gretel – Horse of the Year

WHERE DO THEY GO?

Like people, horses have jobs. Like people, sometimes they enjoy their work and sometimes they tire of it and want something different.

The job of the Saddle Up! horse is very demanding. In a week's time any one horse can have up to fifteen riders, ranging in age from two to nineteen. Those riders also have a wide range of abilities from first-timers to those with more experience and greater skill. Their disabilities may include major physical, cognitive, or verbal limitations; or the riders may be able-bodied but struggle, for example, with anxiety or autism. Some riders need two sidewalkers for support; some, only one. Most lessons are on lead, but a portion of some lessons may include being off lead. A few of the riders are independent, such as the ones in Equestrian Club.

The adjustments each horse needs to repeat over and over again make the job a challenge.

Each horse is screened and trained and goes through a probationary period and then evaluated by instructors and therapists to make sure the fit is right. Many horses serve very well for a period of time—the average is about three years—but then it's time to move on to something different. It's time to say good-bye.

The Moms (the Equine/Farm Director and Assistant) work hard to find a new home that is right for each of the retiring horses. If Hershey could just go down the road from Saddle Up!'s farm, he would find Beau. Beau's original owners welcomed him back when he left Saddle Up! Tommy went to a home where he only has one rider. Together they are doing just fine. When it was clear that J.C. was having issues with intermittent lameness, a volunteer leader at Saddle Up! gave him a new home.

And Gretel? Gretel, a 13.2 hand Haflinger pony, served Saddle Up! riders for nearly nine years. Because of her strength, size, gentle nature, and trustworthiness, she was one of the most used horses for the various programs. In 2014 she was nominated for and won Horse of the Year for PATH International for Region 5.

One of her long-time riders wrote for her nomination: "This horse knows when I am unbalanced and she stops. She is patient and stands still for the mount from my wheelchair. I have been able to do short off-lead walks and on-lead trots only because of her. She is a good horse."

And now Gretel, the good Saddle Up! horse, has another good home, where she is still loved, cared for, and enjoying life.

Volunteers

HERSHEY & THE PAINT JOB

Hershey,—ouch!—here.

Ouch, ouch! Hey! Stop that! I stamped my foot! Getting groomed is supposed to feel good. That hurts! Leader curried again. I stomped harder this time.

Leader got the message and went to get Mom. "He's fine...," I heard him tell her. *Am not!* "...except right here." He showed her. Mom ran her fingers over the spot. She burst out laughing.

"Hershey, have you been helping the volunteers?" She turned to Leader. "Hershey has a paint job! Looks like he must have leaned into the fence they just painted."

She looked at me, "Why'd you do that, silly horse?"

"Not tellin'!" I grumped. But that grass on the other side did taste good.

Volunteering at Saddle Up!

What brings volunteers to Saddle Up? Kids and horses. Horses or kids. It's a toss up.

What keeps volunteers coming back? The experience of Saddle Up! Starting with great training, Saddle Up! extends its caring culture and effectively wraps appreciation and continuing support around each and every volunteer.

Volunteers bring with them a wide range of life experiences. Some have worked with horses or simply loved them from afar. Some have special needs children in their family or have been in school with someone who opened their eyes to see beyond the disability to the person. Some have no past connection with either children with special needs or with horses, but a friend invited them or they read about the program and signed up online.

Some volunteers are retirees, often bringing their grandpa or grandma sensitivities to the children. Some, still in the workforce, nevertheless make time in their busy schedules to also be on the job at Saddle Up! Some are students exploring potential careers in physical, occupational, or recreational therapies or equine-related fields.

Some young adult volunteers are graduates of Saddle Up! After age 19 they come back to give back to the program they love.

Families volunteer. A son or daughter may have a passion for horses, and a parent (or two) is willing to come along—a requirement for volunteers ages 12–15. At 16 the young person can volunteer without that limitation, but often by then the parents are "hooked" and continue to give their time too.

Groups give a day or several at a time. One healthcare corporation in the region sponsors a Day of Service for their employees. They offer numerous sites in the surrounding communities, but on sign-up day all 40 of the slots for Saddle Up! are gone within 10 minutes! The Saddle Up! openings are consistently the first ones filled.

Church youth groups and college students on an "alternative spring break" have weeded and trimmed the landscaping, planted new greenery, created and maintained the trails, built a whole new fence line, and yes, painted fences, much to Hershey's chagrin.

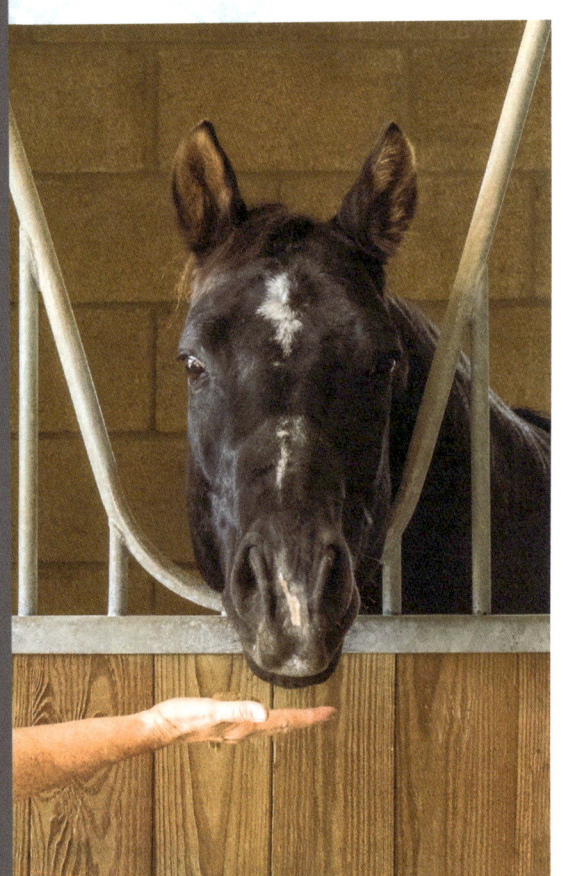

Volunteers often bring special skills too. After serving as a sidewalker and also as a leader and learning more about Saddle Up!, one man put his construction skills to work to remodel a portion of the small barn for use for the Summer Fun Weeks and the school-year EAL lessons. Other volunteers help with administrative needs. Still others serve on the board of Saddle Up!, keeping in mind the big picture and attending to long-range planning.

Saddle Up! volunteers are giving, giving back, and giving more. Without their big hearts and willing hands, Saddle Up! could not exist.

Thank you, Volunteers!

To find out ways you can volunteer, visit the website: saddleupnashville.org.

HERSHEY & TRAINING THE VOLUNTEERS
Hershey, here.

Leader came to the paddock to get me. "Hershey," she says, "today you get to do something special." *Does that mean a treat?* I perk up. We walk through the barn. I try to stop by the Treat Place, but she won't let me. *OK, OK, later.* We turn the corner to go to the crossties. And I plant my feet. I am not moving!

Who are all these people? Where are the kids? These are all grown ups!

"Hershey," she says, "It's OK. These are the new volunteers. They've come for their training. Show them what a good Saddle Up! horse does."

Oh, OK. Into the crossties I go. The people crowd around.

Out come the grooming tools. Leader begins to curry. Round and round. Front to back. *Feels good.* Leader begins to brush. Love it. Someone's talking. I hear "hard brush." The next one's my favorite. *Hurry up and do the soft brush. That's the one. Oh... so nice.*

I'm just really starting to relax when Leader wants to pick my feet. Three of my feet I don't mind—but no, Leader has to start with the one foot I hate to pick up. I don't know why she has to do that one. Three clean feet should be enough, I say. Everyone is watching. I could give Leader a really hard time. *I could. I really could. But... oh, all right—not this time.*

Now the talking just goes on and on and on and on. Leader is still brushing. Not the serious, getting-ready brushing. More the "I know you like this, Hershey" brushing. The eyes are drooping. Talking...talking... Fading....

"Look, Hershey's asleep—standing up!" Someone interrupts my dozing.

I don't bother to open my eyes. Any horse can sleep standing up. I'm just showing the new volunteers what a good Saddle Up! horse does. Staying relaxed in the middle of all that is going on. Waiting patiently for that treat.

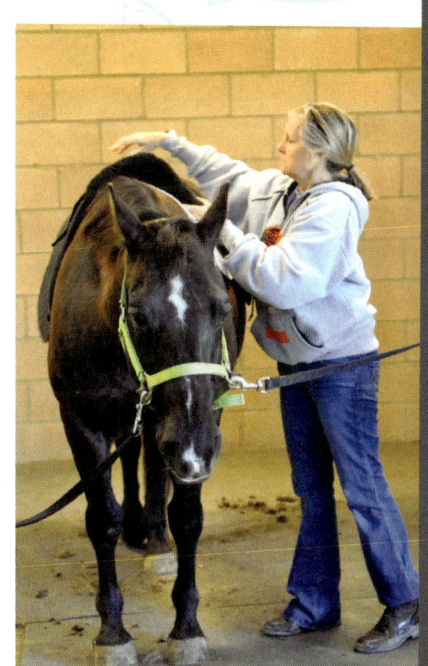

Where all children are equal in the saddle

SLEEPING HORSES

As Hershey says, "Any horse can sleep standing up." A horse can simply "lock" its legs, especially a hind joint (the stifle), drop at the hip, and doze. This unique ability has allowed horses to survive throughout time. In a world of predators and prey, horses are prey. Their primary survival instinct is to run, specifically to *outrun!* Being able to go instantly often makes the difference between life and death for a prey animal.

Horses only sleep two to six hours a day, much of that time standing up. However, they need an average of about thirty minutes each day for the restorative REM (Rapid Eye Movement) sleep. When they feel safe, they will lie down and stretch out, lying on their side like a giant dog. Then, like a dog, they too may twitch, "run," grunt, and even snore in their sleep!

Especially after days of cloudiness, when the sun first comes out, you can find several Saddle Up! horses asleep—either flat out or with their legs tucked under them—soaking up the sun. You'll also see at least one other horse standing—wide awake—on guard for the herd.

Dumpling snoozing in the sun

HERSHEY & THE GHOST

Hershey, here.

My buddy Apache swears there's a ghost in the arena. After a lesson when Apache gets back to our pasture, I hear him tell the nearest horse that will still listen to him (he does this every time) just how brave he was. "That white horse appeared out of nowhere. But I showed it. I laid my ears flat. I shook my head. It was gone—*outathere!*"

I checked around. Nobody else had seen a white horse ghost in the arena. *Get over it, Apache.* (OK, I didn't say that to him. Apache is my buddy. But I did *think* it.)

One day instead of Leader taking me to the crossties, she takes me straight into the arena and turns me loose. *That's different!* I do a quick look-around. No cones, no barrels. Noodles! A big blue thing. Other stuff I'd never seen before. And a lot of people—grown ups, leaning on the rail. *What are they doing here?*

But no one is telling me what to do.

Aha! Now's my chance to look for Apache's ghost.

I head straight to the corner of the arena where Apache says the ghost is. I'm brave. I have ears too!

Apache—there's no white horse ghost!

But there is a black horse. Really good looking! *Oh, I think he likes me.*

I look at him. He looks at me. I move, he moves. *Sweet!* I stretch my black neck out to touch him. He stretches his black neck out. I bump my nose. Something hard! Something cold! I pull back! He pulls back! Was that his nose? *Hmmm...* We try again. I move left. He comes. I move right. (I know left and right—I've been in lots of lessons.) He goes with me. *Yes! I love this horse!*

Funny though, he has no smell.

Leader interrupts. The halter goes on, and I leave my new buddy. I can't wait to get back to tell Apache how *silly* he is!

We walk past the grown ups. They are laughing.

THE BLACK AND WHITE OF IT ALL

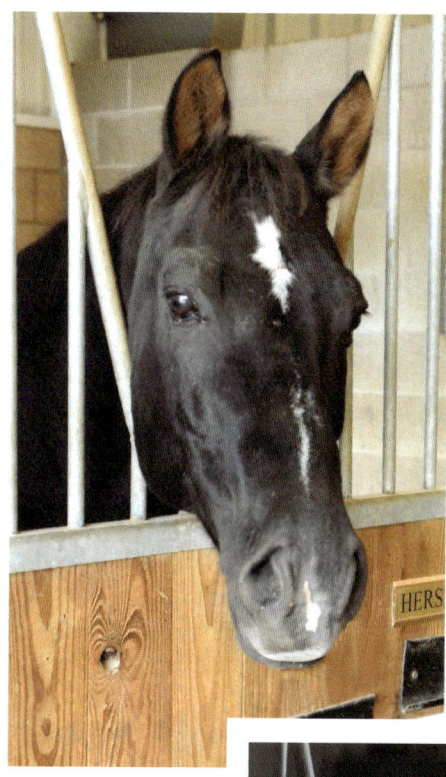

The Saddle Up! herd is an array of color. Some of the horses are white, like Apache. Some are black and "really good looking," as Hershey would say. Of course, Hershey is one of those. If there were any question about it, the big mirrors in the arena don't lie.

Every horse at Saddle Up! has funny little quirks, which endear them to us humans. One of those is that Apache lays his ears back nearly every time he passes one of the mirrors. In "ear talk" he's warning that other horse—"Stay away from me!" Every other horse simply gets used to the mirrors and ignores them. Not Apache.

The day Hershey fell in love with the mirror was another quirky, endearing time. Volunteers, instructors, and other interested grown ups had come to Saddle Up! for a special training session on the traits of the horse. The arena was set up with different items to demonstrate the inquisitive nature of horses. Given things they've not seen before, most horses will tentatively circle, smell, and touch the item lightly and then more playfully as they investigate their environment. Gus, the other horse in that training, was a good example of the expected behavior.

Not Hershey. But then he's not "most" horses!

Where all children are equal in the saddle

Ambassador

HERSHEY & THE MUSIC COUNTRYGRAND PRIX

Hershey, here.

Pal and I were coming back from a good trail ride down by the river. I was already thinking about my treat. But instead of heading for the crossties to be done, Pal took me to the arena. *Hmmm...*

We walked around the arena and then turned in to the Stop-and-Talk Spot. Mom was there. I got a big hug and kiss. (Mom does that sometimes.) She reached down and picked up a pole. I stiffened! There was a flappy thing on it! *Should I run?* She waved it around me. I wanted to run, but Pal held me steady. Pal and Mom kept talking, "Good boy, Hershey. Good boy." *Oh, OK. I get it—no big deal, right?*

I heard music. *OK! We're going to play the Music Game!* I started to walk on, but Pal stopped me. "Stand easy, Hershey. It's not the Music Game this time, Buddy." Pal stroked me and kept talking. We kept standing there. *Hmmm...*

The music stopped, and Pal told me, "Walk on, Hershey." Mom walked on too—with the flappy thing, right beside me. *Definitely not the way to play the Music Game!* Good thing we headed out of the arena.

Bath time! I love a good bath on a warm day. Feels good—and when Pal turns me out in the pasture, I can go roll! That *really* feels good! But no, Pal put me in a stall. Can't roll there. I was stuck in there all night. But I did have plenty of hay.

The next morning Mom came early to let me out. *Good, I can go roll.* But she took me to the round pen and made me walk and trot. I tossed my head a couple of times. *Hey! Let me go run around in my pasture! I want to roll!*

Back to the crossties. Extra grooming. "Hershey, you shine!" Mom clipped on my lead, and we started to leave the barn. *Now, I'll get a good roll.*

Oh, no, the trailer! She wasn't taking me to my pasture. The last time I was in the trailer, I left all my buddies and never saw them again. *Was I leaving Saddle Up!? Would I ever see Harley and Lacy and the others again? Would I ever see Riders or Pal again?*

At least there was plenty hay in the trailer. And Apache. *Hmmm...*

When the trailer door finally opened, Mom came to get me. "Hershey, look at you—you have hay on your face!" I backed out. I looked around. I stiffened. *What was this place?* I looked again. Whew! Rider was there. Leader and Sidewalkers too. Lots of horses—strangers. *Apache, what's going on?* Busy, busy. Noisy too.

Rider up! "Ready, Hershey? It's just like you practiced. You'll be fine." Mom gave me a kiss. Then she gave Sidewalker the flappy thing! Apache got a kiss too—and another flappy thing. *Hmmm...*

Our leaders took us to an arena. I knew it was an arena, but it was

Where all children are equal in the saddle

really different. No cones. No mailbox. No basketball thing. Big walls. Big poles high off the ground. Lots of little flappy things. And one horse. I watched. That horse was headed straight for the wall! *Oh, my!* He just flew over it. And then again. And again. *Oh my!* People were clapping and cheering. *Oh, my!*

The gate opened. Rider said, "Walk on, Hershey." I did. *Would I have to jump over those fences?* Apache and I walked around the edge of the arena, past all the people. They were quiet. I could hear the big voice. It said my name. I *know* my name. We went to the Stop-and-Talk Spot—every arena has one. The people all stood up. The music began. *OK, Mom. I remember—just like we practiced.*

The music stopped. The people cheered! *For me?*

"Walk on, Hershey, walk on." Out of the arena, back to the trailer with Apache, and yes, back to Saddle Up! Finally, back to my pasture.

Ahhh... nothing like a really good roll!

SADDLE UP! AMBASSADOR

Horses are a lot like people. When they are doing a job that jives with who they are, they are indeed happy. At Saddle Up! Hershey is known as "Mr. Versatility." He's happy not only on the trail but also in the arena. He willingly does the Therapeutic Riding lessons, Equestrian Club, Therapy Services, EAL, the Summer Fun Week programs, and fundraising.

Fundraising?

Yes. Unlike cars, which when they are parked aren't costing owners any gas money, all 24 of Saddle Up!'s horses need to eat all the time, including their days off. The benefits of Saddle Up!'s programs are immeasurable, but the costs are not only measurable but also relentless.

The cost for a lesson is $150 each time. Yet the families of the children pay only $25 of that, and many families receive scholarships. Seventy-six percent (76%) of all funds raised go to support the programs. Fifteen percent (15%) is invested in fundraising, and only nine percent (9%) goes to management.

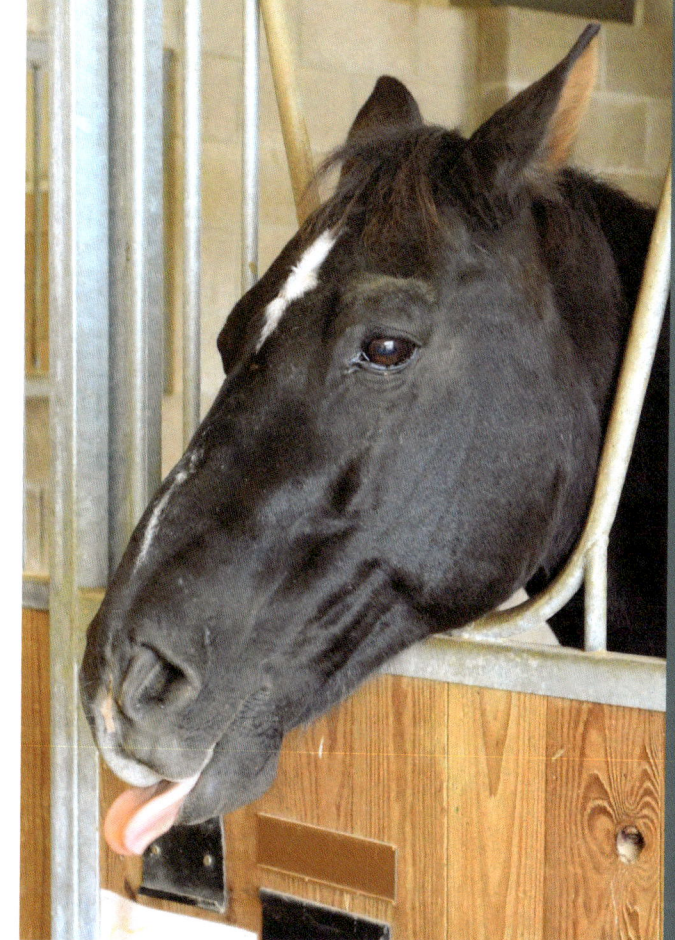

Little or big—they have to eat!

Where all children are equal in the saddle

Where do the funds come from?

First, from individuals and volunteers. Thirty-six percent (36%) of the annual cost is covered by donations from people who care about children with disabilities and who love horses. They give their support through dollars. The 500-plus volunteers support the mission of Saddle Up! with their time, contributing in 2014 alone 17,448 hours—the equivalent of $392,580 (based on the national value per hour of volunteer time). The fees for riding lessons, therapy services, and other programs that the families pay contributes 16% to the budget; grants and other miscellaneous sources account for 18%.

The remaining 30% comes from events, such as the 5K and Fun Run organized by Saddle Up!'s youngest supporters: the children of a nearby elementary school. Nearly 300 people participated in the run, and the school raised $10,000 for Saddle Up! In the tradition of Music City, Nashville-based recording artists have also donated time, delighting attendees with their music and their heart for Saddle Up!'s children and horses.

The biggest events, however, are Chukkers for Charity (a world-class polo match) and the Music Country Grand Prix, where Hershey was one of the equine ambassadors, introducing horse lovers who had come to watch world-class show jumpers compete over the big fences to the world-class program called Saddle Up!

At both events two horses and two Saddle Up! riders with their teams of leader and sidewalkers enter the arena bringing the American flag. The announcer tells the crowd about Saddle Up! and introduces the riders and horses. (Yes, Hershey did hear his name.)

Then the audience stands and sings the National Anthem. They cheer too—because in the riders they have a new image of what it means to be free and to be brave with the assistance of horses like Hershey, who have found the right job.

Just don't ask him to jump!

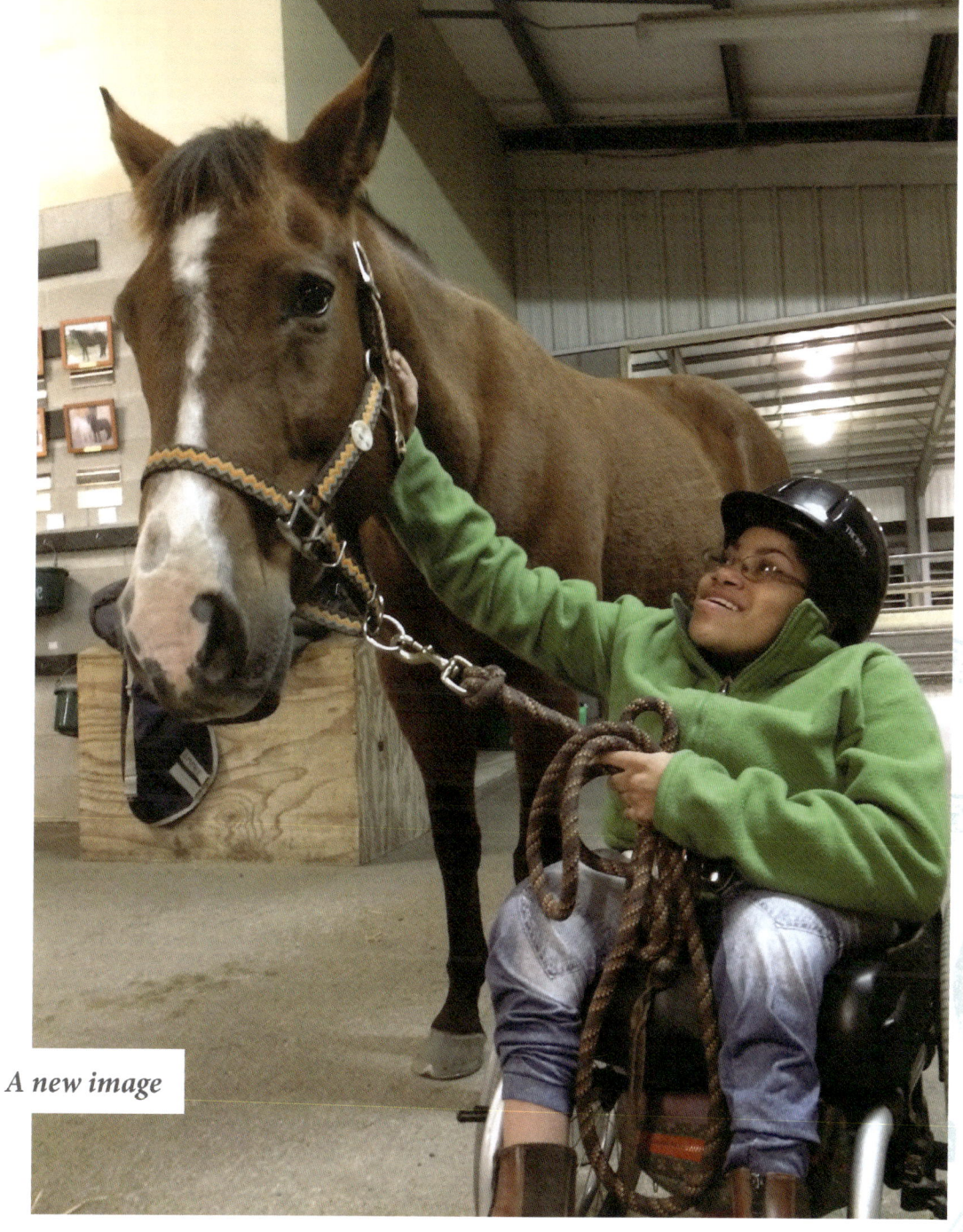

A new image

Where all children are equal in the saddle

A WIN/WIN!

Every year, two big events showcase the amazing versatility, beauty, and athleticism of horses—and proceeds help fund Saddle Up! If you love horses and Saddle Up!, mark your calendar for either or both of these champion competitions:

Chukkers for Charity Polo Match

This prestigious polo competition brings in top-ranked national and international teams and riders for a fast-paced, edge-of-your-seat game. It is held in September. Visit the website for more information: chukkersforcharity.net.

Music Country Grand Prix

This premier equestrian show jumping competition features top riders and horses from across the nation. It is held in late May or early June. Visit the website for more information: musiccountrygrandprix.com.

Where all children are equal in the saddle

HERSHEY BAR, VIDEO STAR

If Hershey were to tell you about the day he was filmed for Saddle Up!'s video, he'd only be able to talk about "the lady with the big black thing who kept showing up" wherever he was during the SUPER Show. But what Hershey doesn't know is more remarkable than what he does.

Hershey doesn't know that, thanks to the lady with the big black video camera, people around the country and even across the seas know him. They've seen him on Saddle Up!'s website's home page and on YouTube! Hershey Bar is a video star!

The 15-time Emmy award winning Demetria Kalodimos, who is also the long-time evening news anchor for Nashville's NBC affiliate, produced the video through her own company, Genuine Human Productions. The tagline of Genuine Human Productions is "Real People - True Stories." As Saddle Up!'s star ambassador, Hershey would lobby for "Real People - *Great Horses!* - True Stories." After all, the Saddle Up! story isn't complete without the horses. Let him show you:

Saddle Up!'s website home page: saddleupnashville.org

or

YouTube: "It's Pretty Out Here," http://youtu.be/AOc0IpjSFDg

Saddle Up!'s mission is to provide children and youth with disabilities the opportunity to grow and develop through therapeutic, educational, and recreational activities with horses.

We invite you to support Saddle Up! in that mission.

Please visit our website:

saddleupnashville.org

To learn more about Saddle Up! and how to volunteer or contribute.*
*Your contributions are tax deductable and very much appreciated.

Contact us:
615-794-1150
info@saddleupnashville.org
or consult the list of email addresses that are on the website.

Or visit us at the farm:

Saddle Up!
1549 Old Hillsboro Road
Franklin, TN 37069-9136

PATH to Excellence

Founded in 1969, today PATH International (Professional Association of Therapeutic Horsemanship International) has more than 850 member centers all over the world, serving more than 58,000 children, youth, and adults with physical, cognitive, and emotional needs through a variety of equine-assisted activities and therapies. The organization certifies instructors, accredits centers, provides educational opportunities, and advocates for the growth and professionalism of equine-related services for persons with special needs.

To be certified by PATH, instructors must attend workshops, pass a written exam, and demonstrate their practical skills in two different types of demonstration lessons. All of Saddle Up!'s instructors have achieved certification; several have earned the advanced level.

PATH also conducts site visits regularly. As a facility and program, Saddle Up! has attained the highest level of accreditation, Premier Accredited Center, which fewer than one-third of the centers achieve. As such, Saddle Up! is also a source for mentoring other programs and can provide opportunities for interns to learn and grow.

Working to retain these designations year after year demonstrates Saddle Up!'s commitment to the safety, ethical practices, professionalism, and effectiveness that the PATH standards represent.

Add to those qualities the passion for children and the love of horses, and all together that's what makes Saddle Up! so excellent!

Visit www.pathintl.org for more information about PATH or to find a program like Saddle Up! in your area.

THANK YOU!

Hershey is the real name of a real horse, but I want to give a thank you the Hershey Corporation. I can't imagine any other name for our hero. Hershey is indeed that dark chocolate—good for you—sweet treat people think of when they hear the name "Hershey." Milton Hershey, who not only created our favorite chocolate treats, also established a home and school, which has cared for disadvantaged and orphaned children since 1909, helping them "gain the skills to be successful in all aspects of life." (Sounds like Saddle Up!) Mr. Hershey would be proud of his equine namesake.

Staff and volunteers have given their time to tell me these stories—there are so many, every one of them inspiring! They have also given their time to read the manuscript to help me write the stories the best way possible. So a special thank you to Marty Foy, Lynne Evans, Heather Silverman, Morgan Plunkett, Susan Lutz, Julie Upshur, Kim Kline, Samantha Bell, Sandra Zaccari, Kelley Newman, Jennifer Krause, Kristina Wilson, Martha Ann Pilcher, and Cheryl Scutt. I knew I could count on their passion and generosity—that's just who Saddle Up! people are!

A special thank you also to Lynn Vincent who gave me hope and who also led me to Marcia Myatt. Marcia donated her time and skill, designing the book and covers, to bring the stories to life. I am truly grateful!

My husband of fifty years, Ed, and my daughter, Ellen, also get my most heartfelt thanks. They've not only put up with but also encouraged my passion for horses and for Saddle Up! Through the years they've also been quick to say, "Mom, go ride your horse. You'll be a nicer person!" Yes, riding is therapeutic for me too.

Thank you too, dear Reader, for purchasing this book. I have gained so much from being with horses, and I have seen through my years of volunteering at Saddle Up! how much the horses give to the children. I want to help Saddle Up! continue its mission. Writing this book has been a labor of love. Profits from its sales go to support the wonderful work done at Saddle Up!

—Crys Zinkiewicz

CPSIA information can be obtained at www.ICGtesting.com
Printed in the USA
LVIW01n2106170416
484055LV00006B/13